HISTORY MATTERS

A wider world
The making of the United Kingdom:1500-1750

Rosemary Kelly

Stanley Thornes (Publishers) Ltd

Acknowledgements

A textbook of this nature owes a great debt to numbers of distinguished historians. The author, however, would like to acknowledge the following in particular:

D. Cook, *Documents and Debates: Sixteenth-century England* (Macmillan, 1980) for Source 2J
A. Fraser, *The Weaker Vessel* (Methuen, 1984) for information on women in the Civil War in Chapter 5
G.H. Jenkins, *Discovering Welsh History: 3* (OUP, 1989) for material on the Welsh Bible in Chapter 2
M. Pearce and G. Stewart, *Sources in History: Sixteenth Century* (Unwin Hyman, 1988) for Sources 3N and 3P
M. Pearce and G. Stewart, *Sources in History: Seventeenth Century* (Unwin Hyman, 1988) for map on the extent of the plague and fire which has been simplified for page 65 of this book
J. Pound, *Poverty and Vagrancy in Tudor England* (Longman, 1971) for material on the Norwich census in Chapter 3 and poverty generally
A. Raine (ed.), *York Civic Records* (Yorkshire Archaeological Society, 1939) for York regulations in Chapter 1
M. Rule, *The Mary Rose: Excavation and Raising of Henry VIII's Flagship* (Conway Maritime Press, 1982) for Sources C and D on page 5 and information on the *Mary Rose* in 'Setting the Scene'
J. Wormald (ed.), *Scotland Revisited* (Collins and Brown, 1991) for material on Scotland in Chapter 1

The author is also very grateful to David Grace, Head of History, Beaufort School, Gloucester, for valuable advice on the structure and approach of this book, and to Joan Dils, Tutor, University of Oxford Department for Continuing Education, for information on St Giles's Church, Reading.

The author and publishers are grateful to the following for permission to reproduce photographs:
Ancient Art and Architecture Collection: pages 20; 63(b) • Robert Ashby: page 69(b) • Ashmolean Museum, Oxford: page 57(t) • Bridgeman Art Library: pages 4, Thyssen–Bornemisza Collection, Lugano–Castagnola; 8(b), Galleria dell'Academia, Venice; 9(b), National Gallery, London; 14, Hatfield House, Hertfordshire; 26(t); 36; 56; 68; Private Collections; 62, Roy Miles Fine Paintings, London; 69(t), Sir John Soane Museum, London; 77, National Gallery, London • British Library, London: pages 7; 9(t); 16(t); 22; 55(b) • Reproduced by Courtesy of the Trustees of the British Museum: pages 26(b); 49(b) • The College of Arms, Westminster Tournament Roll: page 10 • Country Life Library: page 34 • Crown Copyright material in the PRO, reproduced by permission of the Controller of HMSO: page 33 • E.T. Archive: pages 4–5(b) • Mary Evans Picture Library: pages 15(t); 25 • Fotomas Index: pages 38(tl and b); 44; 47; 49(t); 52; 53(b); 59(r); 66(br) • Freer Gallery of Art, Smithsonian Institute, Washington: page 74 • Glasgow Museums and Art Galleries: page 32(l) • Great Scot Pictures: page 13 • Michael Holford: page 72(tl) • Hulton–Deutsch Collection: page 46 • Kupferstichkabinett der Oeffentlichen Kunstsammlung, Basel: page 24 • Magdalene College, Cambridge: page 64 • Mansell Collection: pages 15(b); 16(b); 17; 21; 27; 32(r); 38; 39; 40 (all); 43 (both); 50; 57(b); 58; 59(l); 61; 63(t); 65; 66(bl) • Mary Rose Trust: page 6 (both) • Reproduced by courtesy of the Trustees of the National Library of Scotland and Sir David Ogilvy: page 12 • National Maritime Museum, Greenwich: page 37 • National Portrait Gallery, London: pages 18 (both); 19; 30; 31; 35; 41; 48; 53(t); 55(t); 60; 66(t); 73 • National Trust Photographic Library, York: page 23 • Ann Ronan Picture Library: page 76(l) • Royal Collection, St James's Palace, © Her Majesty the Queen: pages 45; 71, cover • Trustees of the Science Museum, London: page 76(r) • Scottish National Portrait Gallery: page 70 • Trustees of the Victoria and Albert Museum, London: page 42.

Every effort has been made to contact copyright holders and we apologise if any have been overlooked.

Text © Rosemary Kelly 1992

Original line illustrations © Stanley Thornes (Publishers) Ltd 1992 (maps and charts by Barking Dog Art, other illustrations by Tim Hayward)
Picture research by Juliet Duff
Designed by Glynis Edwards

All rights reserved. No part of this publication may be reproduced or transmitted in any form or by any means, electronic or mechanical, including photocopy, recording or any information storage and retrieval system, without permission in writing from the publisher or under licence from the Copyright Licensing Agency Limited. Further details of such licences (for reprographic reproduction) may be obtained from the Copyright Licensing Agency Limited, of 90 Tottenham Court Road, London W1P 9HE.

First published in 1992 by:
Stanley Thornes (Publishers) Ltd
Old Station Drive
Leckhampton
CHELTENHAM   GL53 0DN
England

Reprinted 1992

A catalogue record for this book is available
from the British Library.
ISBN 0–7487–1235–6

Typeset by Tech-Set, Gateshead, Tyne & Wear.
Printed and bound in Hong Kong.

The picture on the cover shows kings at their grandest – part of the painting of 'The Field of the Cloth of Gold', when Henry VIII met the King of France in 1520. Thomas Wolsey, the King's chief minister organised it all – he rides beside the King in the inset picture, top left. There are many scenes in the picture: the Kings meet in the golden tent (left background), and watch a joust (right background). In front of the palace in the centre (specially built for the occasion) local people make the most of the free wine running from the fountains.

Contents

Setting the scene   4
Shipwreck! An investigation • Britain in a wider world

Chapter 1   The people of Britain   10
The second Tudor king • The four nations in Britain • Knowing your place • People and change

Chapter 2   Church and people   18
The King's 'Great Matter' • The Reformation in Europe • A Bible people could understand • The end of the monasteries • Challenges to Henry VIII • Protestant king and Catholic queen • The middle way

Chapter 3   Elizabeth I and her world   30
The Queen and her court • A queen in Scotland • Threats at home – 'The monstrous huge dragon' • Threats abroad – Danger from Spain • The Armada • Crime, punishment and poverty • Elizabethans enjoy themselves

Chapter 4   Crown and Parliament   42
James I • The Gunpowder Plot, 1605 • Puritans and pilgrims • Charles I • Eleven years without Parliament • Steps to war

Chapter 5   Cavaliers and Roundheads   50
The two sides • England in 1642 • Experiences of war • Oliver Cromwell and the Ironsides • Trial and execution • Sword rule

Chapter 6   Rulers and revolution   62
A king again • Changing Europe • Plague and fire • 1688 – It looks like revolution • The United Kingdom of Britain

Chapter 7   A wider world   71
The new London • New goods to buy • 'The great ocean of truth' • Mr and Mrs Andrews • Summing up: 1500–1750

Index/Glossary   80

How to use this book

When you study History you go on a journey of discovery into the past, and you need skills to find the way. This book helps you to learn these skills, and make your own discoveries, by aiming for:

Attainment Target 1: Understanding the past, especially: change, and continuity (what did not change); causes – why things happened; results – the effect they had; what it was like to live in times when people's beliefs, attitudes, and experiences were very different from our own.
Attainment Target 2: Understanding that people in the past, and people now, can look at past events in different ways, and why this happens.
Attainment Target 3: Finding and testing evidence from many different sources. The section called *Shipwreck!* on page 4 helps you to work out ways of reaching this target.

Written sources (what people at the time said and wrote) give important and interesting evidence, but old-fashioned English can be difficult to understand. So simpler words have sometimes been used, and complicated bits left out, but the meaning has not been altered.

Questions help you to understand what you have read, and to reach the three attainment targets. Most questions have the number of the target you are aiming at, shown like this $^{AT}_{1.4}$

Flashbacks are signs like this ◁☐. They refer to earlier pages, and help you to link up what you have learnt, and remember it.

The index on page 80 includes a **glossary** which explains important words which may be difficult or unfamiliar.

Money in the Early Modern Age

In old money: 20 shillings (20s) = £1

1 shilling = 12 old pennies (12d)

The value of money is very different now, so it does not help to turn these sums into modern money. It is useful to know:

The average daily wage for a labourer in the 1500s was 5d and in the 1600s, 1s.

The average cost of running a Tudor nobleman's household for a year: £1,000.

Setting the scene

Shipwreck! An investigation

Henry VIII was proud of being a warlike king. He went to war against England's two old enemies, France and Scotland, three times – which cost a lot of money and gained him very little. One expense was the great warships built in his reign. The *Mary Rose* was his second largest ship, called after his younger sister. (He called the biggest one after himself.)

On 19 July 1545, a French invasion fleet approached Portsmouth, the King's most important naval base on the south coast. It was a calm sunny day. Henry VIII stood watching proudly on the shore, as his fleet sailed out from Portsmouth harbour to attack the French ships.

The *Mary Rose* was crammed, with about 600 soldiers and 100 sailors on board. Sir Peter Carew's eyewitness account (see opposite) says that the sailors were experienced men who would not take orders from each other, and were squabbling about what should be done as the ship prepared for battle. The ship's gunports were open, with her 91 guns ready to fire.

Suddenly, as the sails were going up, the great ship heeled right over. Water poured into the open gunports on that side, and the heavy guns broke

SOURCE A Henry VIII (1509–47), painted in 1537 by the King's great artist Hans Holbein. Holbein used real gold on the King's costume, and the silk, fur and jewels look as if you could touch them. Above all he showed the character of the people he painted. What kind of person does Henry seem to be?

SETTING THE SCENE

free of their lashings, sliding across the lower decks, and tipping the ship even further. She capsized, and sank so quickly that only about 40 men were saved. The King could hear the desperate cries of the drowning crew from the shore. By his side, Lady Carew, the wife of the commander, fell in a dead faint as she saw her husband's ship go down.

Meanwhile, the battle between the English and French came to nothing, and after some unpleasant raids on the south coast, the French fleet sailed home.

The Mary Rose – Tudor Time Capsule

For over 400 years, the *Mary Rose* lay deep in the mud of the Solent (the sea channel between Portsmouth and the Isle of Wight). From 1971, a team of archaeologist divers worked under water on the wreck for eleven years, recording and measuring everything they found, and bringing up what they could. At last in 1982, a huge crane hauled up the actual ship. Now everyone can see the ship, and the things found in her, in the *Mary Rose* Museum in Portsmouth.

Why did she sink? Two eyewitness accounts

> **SOURCE C**
>
> The weather favoured our attempt for it was a perfect calm. Our galleys [big armed rowing boats] had all the advantage we could desire, to the great damage of the English who for want of wind lay exposed to our cannon. The *Mary Rose*, one of their principal ships, was sunk by our cannon and of 5 or 600 men which were on board, only 5 and 30 escaped.
>
> The Admiral who commanded the French invasion fleet

> **SOURCE B** In Henry VIII's illustrated list of his warships, the 'Mary Rose' is painted ready for battle. She bristled with guns poking out of the open gunports along her sides. Notice how close some gunports are to the water

> **SOURCE D**
>
> Sir George Carew commanded every man to take his place and the sails to be hoist but the *Mary Rose* began to heel, that is to lean over to one side. Then the commander of another ship called to Sir George, asking him how he did, who answered he had the sort of knaves whom he could not rule, and it was not long after that the said Mary Rose, thus heeling more and more, was drowned with 700 men which were in her, with very few escaped.
>
> Sir Peter Carew, brother of Sir George Carew, the commander of the *Mary Rose*. He was with the King when the ship sank.

1. What reasons do Sources C and D give for the sinking of the 'Mary Rose'? — AT 3.3
2. What information does each source give about the numbers on board? Which account is more likely to be accurate? — AT 3.5
3. What did Sir George Carew mean when he said he 'had the sort of knaves whom he could not rule'? — AT 3.3
4. The archaeologists found nothing to prove the account in Source C. What might they have found if it was true? Which are facts and which are opinions in this account? — AT 2.3
5. Use Sources B, C, and D to decide why you think the 'Mary Rose' sank, and explain how you have made up your mind. — AT 3.5

A WIDER WORLD

Life on board a Tudor warship

> **SOURCE E**
>
> **Some objects found in the *Mary Rose***
>
> The bones of the men trapped in the ship; the skeleton of a small dog, near a skeleton of a rat it was chasing; the skeleton of a frog; Tudor flies, beetles and cockroaches.
>
> Guns of different sizes; longbows and arrows.
>
> Beef, venison (deer meat) and mutton bones cut into serving portions; plum stones; peas in the pod; herbs and spices; plates and leather bottles.
>
> The surgeon's medicine chest: it had tweezers, a syringe, medicine and ointment jars, bottles, basins, bandages, razors, and a mallet.
>
> The surgeon's velvet cap 80▷; a pair of fashionable knee length boots; shoes; knitted stockings; leather jerkins.
>
> A trumpet; tabors (small drums); pieces of stringed instruments; a backgammon board and pieces; dice.

6 Which object shows when the 'Mary Rose' was built? Why did every ship have this important item? *AT 3.4*

7 The objects in Source E are arranged in groups. What does each group, and Source G, tell you about life on the 'Mary Rose', and the people who used the objects? *AT 3.3*

Do sources tell the whole story?

One source hardly ever tells the whole story. The *Mary Rose* tells us about life on a Tudor warship in 1545, but most people in Tudor Britain never went near a warship. Sometimes in a written source, the writer leaves things out on purpose, or because they do not know about them. Historians study as many different sources as possible to find evidence of the past.

8 Taking sides in History is called bias. Are Sources C and D biased? Does that make them useless? Explain your opinion. *AT 3.8*

9 What impression of Henry VIII do these sources give? *AT 3.4*

10 How many different kinds of source have you studied on these pages? Suggest other kinds of source which give us historical evidence.

SOURCE F A bell found on the 'Mary Rose', used to ring for the 'watch' – the time members of the crew started or finished their hours on duty. The writing round the top is in Flemish. It says 'I was made in 1510'

SOURCE G More objects found on the 'Mary Rose'

Fine leather pouch, with IHS on it – the Christian sign for Jesus
Wooden seal used to stamp wax with a coat of arms
Trade tokens
Wooden whistle
Pocket sundial
A die
Rosary 80▷
Comb used to get rid of lice
Thimble ring
Decorated clasp

SETTING THE SCENE

Britain in a wider world

Here are some important questions which this book helps you to investigate. They are mostly about changes which have helped to shape our modern world. They help to explain why historians call this time from about 1500 to 1750 the Early Modern Age.

Power: Kings like Henry VIII seem very powerful. So how was it that a century later an English king was put on trial and beheaded in public? Were rulers less powerful after that?

Nationality: By 1750, the four separate nations in Britain – Scots, English, Welsh and Irish – were one united kingdom. How did this come about, and were they really one nation?

Religion: When the *Mary Rose* sank, the Catholic Church in Europe was splitting up. How did this affect powerful people like kings, bishops and nobles, and ordinary people too?

A wider world: Henry VIII's ships never sailed far from the English coast. But look at the map below. Britain was part of a much wider world, and Spanish and Portuguese explorers were already beginning to discover parts of it. Britain caught up later. By 1750, she was a rich trading nation, in contact with cultures very different from her own. What problems and challenges did this change bring?

11 Compare Source H with a modern map of the world, taking each continent in turn. What does it tell you about European discoveries in the rest of the world at this time?

AT 3.5

SOURCE H   A map like this probably decorated the ceiling of a building specially designed for Henry VIII for a grand peace-making ceremony with the King of France in 1527. It gives us a good idea of what educated Europeans knew about the rest of the world then

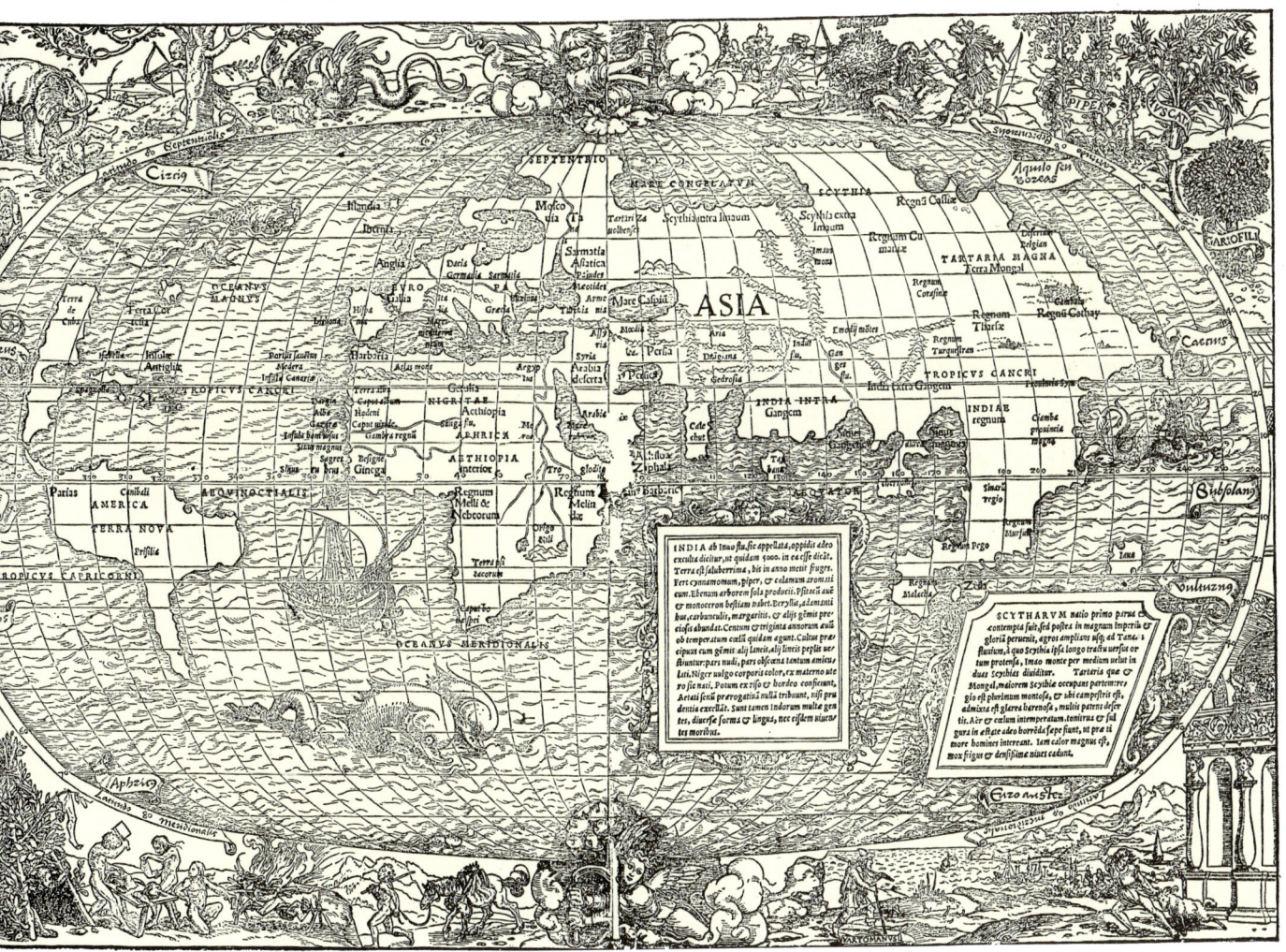

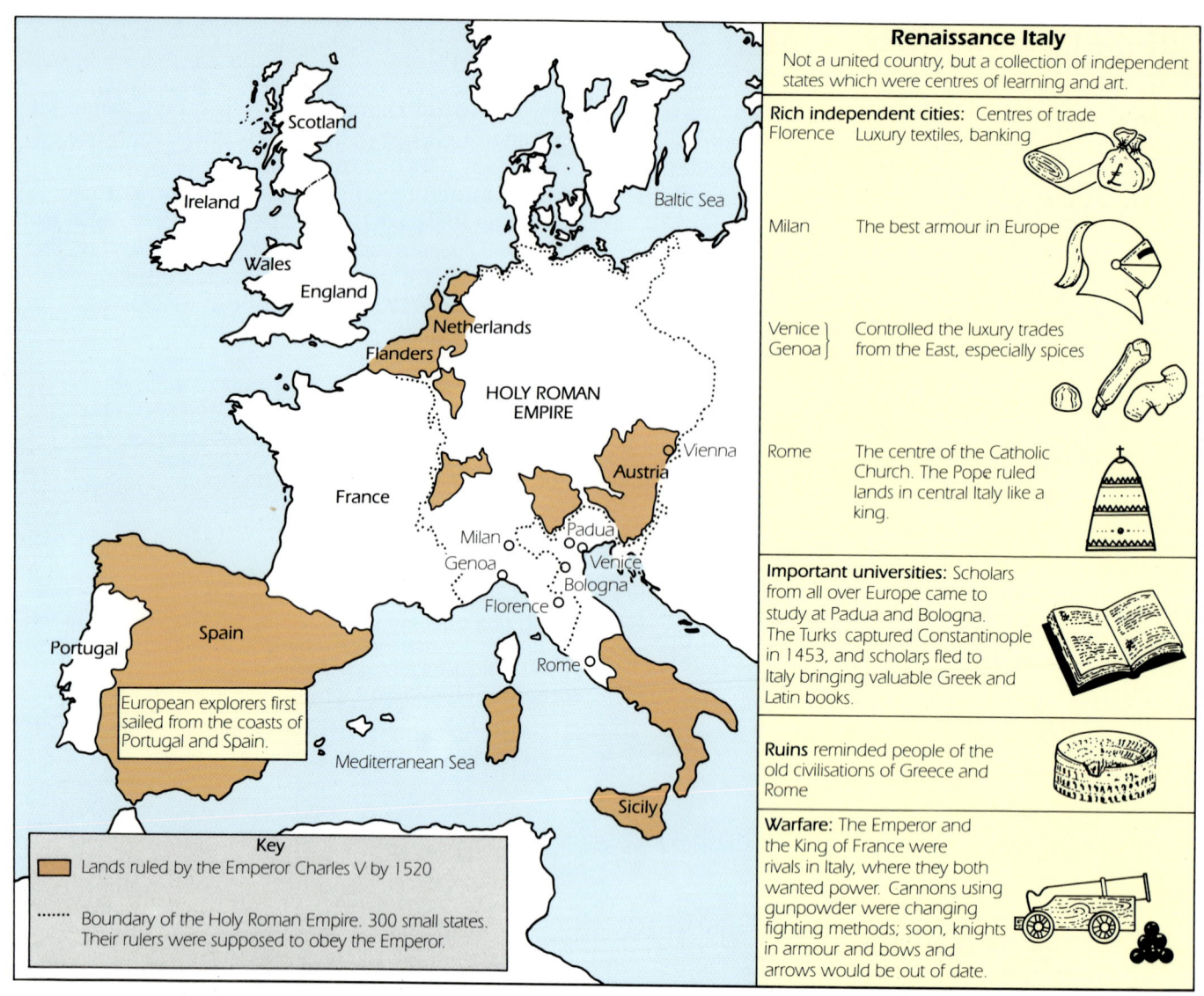

A WIDER WORLD

Renaissance Italy
Not a united country, but a collection of independent states which were centres of learning and art.

Rich independent cities: Centres of trade

Florence	Luxury textiles, banking
Milan	The best armour in Europe
Venice / Genoa	Controlled the luxury trades from the East, especially spices
Rome	The centre of the Catholic Church. The Pope ruled lands in central Italy like a king.

Important universities: Scholars from all over Europe came to study at Padua and Bologna. The Turks captured Constantinople in 1453, and scholars fled to Italy bringing valuable Greek and Latin books.

Ruins reminded people of the old civilisations of Greece and Rome.

Warfare: The Emperor and the King of France were rivals in Italy, where they both wanted power. Cannons using gunpowder were changing fighting methods; soon, knights in armour and bows and arrows would be out of date.

European explorers first sailed from the coasts of Portugal and Spain.

Key
- Lands ruled by the Emperor Charles V by 1520
- .... Boundary of the Holy Roman Empire. 300 small states. Their rulers were supposed to obey the Emperor.

Britain and Europe, about 1520

The Renaissance means rebirth. The name is used for the surge of new ideas which began in Italy, and spread in Europe as educated people discovered more about themselves and the world they lived in, and looked back to the old civilisations of Greece and Rome as the key to exciting new discoveries.

Leonardo Da Vinci (1452–1519) is one of the most interesting men of the Renaissance. He was a painter, sculptor, architect, poet and scientist. His notebooks record his observations of plants and animals, the human body, buildings and machines – he even tried to invent a flying machine.

12 What do you think was the biggest problem for the Emperor Charles V? Do you think he was usually stronger than the King of France? *AT 1.3*

13 Why did Italy become a centre of learning and art? *AT 1.4*

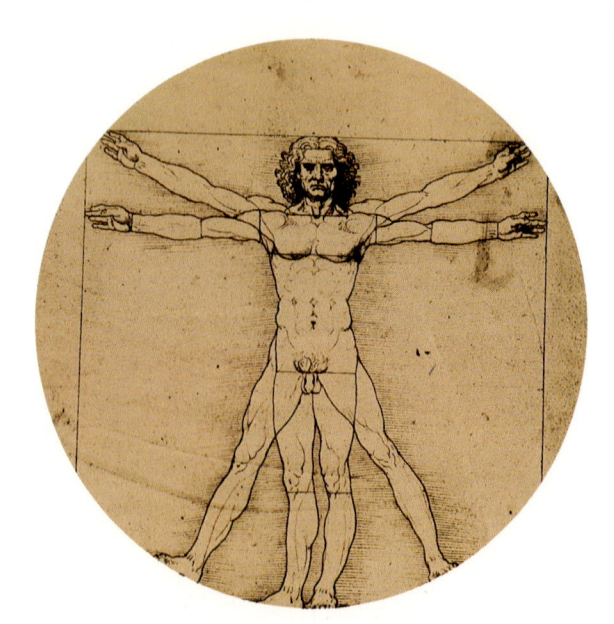

A sketch from Leonardo's notebooks. He is working out the proportions of the human figure

SETTING THE SCENE

Artists explore space

Artists have painted the Virgin Mary and the child Jesus for centuries. These two pictures show the different ways two artists painted this special mother and child. Source I was painted and decorated beautifully in gold by an unknown monk in about 1310, before most artists had begun to discover how to make space in their pictures. Leonardo Da Vinci painted Source J, *The Virgin of the Rocks*, in 1506. By then, artists were interested in other subjects as well – as the mysterious background shows. The Virgin Mary stretches out her hands to John the Baptist and Jesus, while an angel watches over them.

14 Compare the two paintings by answering these questions: How has each artist painted Mary and Jesus? Can you tell whether Mary is sitting or standing, and if so how? What is the background like? Do you think one picture is better than the other, or are they just different? *(AT 1.3)*

SOURCE I

An invention which changed the world

In the Middle Ages, books were handwritten on parchment, and were so rare and expensive they were kept chained up.

In 1460, the first printing press was set up in Europe – in Mainz, Germany. It copied a method of making moveable type which the Chinese had used for over 700 years. Europeans also copied another Chinese invention – making paper cheaply from rags and vegetable matter, instead of using expensive parchment.

1476: William Caxton, a rich London merchant, set up the first printing press in Westminster.
1508: Andrew Millar (his name tells you his trade) started the first Scottish press in Edinburgh.

By then, there were at least 20 printing presses in Europe, and 20 million books had been produced.

15 What were the problems when there were only hand-written books? *(AT 1.4)*

16 Why were printed books cheaper than handwritten ones? *(AT 1.3)*

17 How many times have you read printed words today? (Think about food packets, instructions, advertisements, books, etc.) Now write down as many reasons as you can why printing was such an important invention. Share your ideas with the class. *(AT 1.4)*

SOURCE J

1 The people of Britain

The second Tudor king

Henry VIII was lucky when he became king in 1509. He was 18, just old enough to rule, and it was exciting to have a new young ruler. His father, Henry VII, had become king because he won the Battle of Bosworth in 1485, and spent his reign making his throne secure. He was not popular when he died – he was too good at collecting taxes and fines – but he left:

- a peaceful country
- enough money to run the country for two years
- good marriages for three of his children:

Arthur married **Catherine of Aragon,** daughter of the King of Spain. Arthur died aged 16, soon after the marriage.

Henry VIII married **Catherine of Aragon** when he became King, to carry out his father's wishes.

Margaret married **James IV of Scotland.** This marriage was arranged to bring peace between England and Scotland. 79▷

Henry VIII enjoyed being a king. He loved ceremonies and banquets, and the rich clothes and jewels that went with them. By the end of his reign he owned 55 palaces. He went on making a good impression too:

SOURCE 1A

His Majesty is 29 years old and extremely handsome, very fair, and his whole frame admirably proportioned; he has a beard that looks like gold. He is a good musician, composes well, is a most skilful horseman, a fine jouster, speaks good French, Latin and Spanish. He is very religious, and very fond of hunting. He is extremely fond of tennis, at which it is the prettiest thing in the world to see him play, his fair skin glowing through his shirt.

The ambassador from Venice, to his rulers at home

SOURCE 1B
Young King Henry jousts before Queen Catherine, proudly displaying both their initials. They are celebrating the birth of their son, though sadly the baby soon died. Henry thunders down on his opponent on the other side of the barrier. He was a good jouster, though courtiers found it tactful to let him win

INVESTIGATIONS

What were rulers expected to be like?
How did people live in Tudor Britain?

Key Sources
- Pictures painted or printed at the time
- James IV's accounts
- Fitzherbert's *Book of Husbandry* (farming)
- Regulations in York

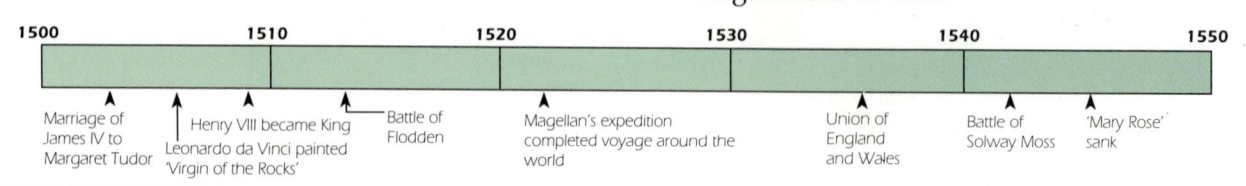

Timeline 1500–1550

- Marriage of James IV to Margaret Tudor
- Leonardo da Vinci painted 'Virgin of the Rocks'
- Henry VIII became King
- Battle of Flodden
- Magellan's expedition completed voyage around the world
- Union of England and Wales
- Battle of Solway Moss
- 'Mary Rose' sank

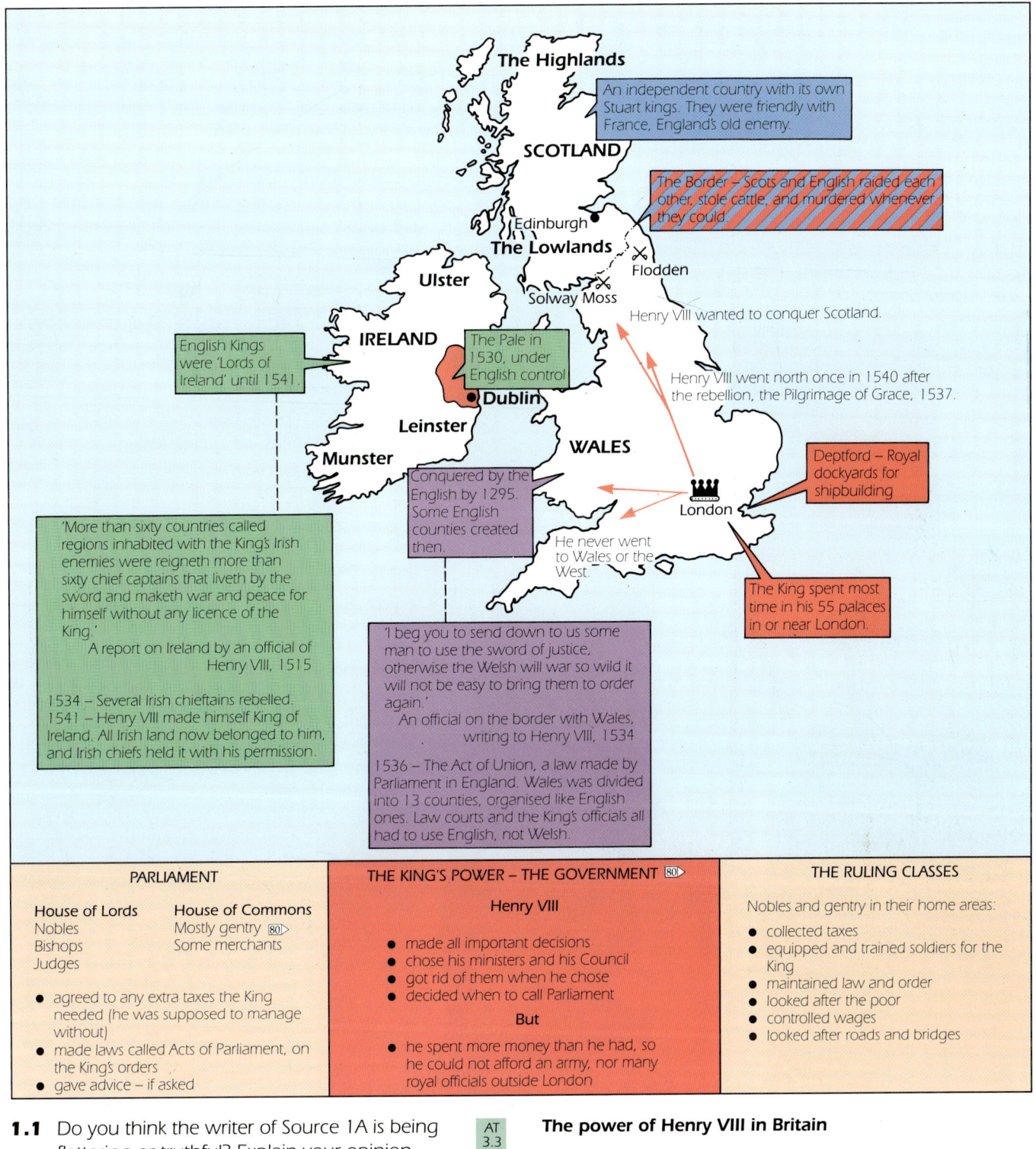

THE PEOPLE OF BRITAIN

Map of Britain and Ireland

The Highlands

SCOTLAND — An independent country with its own Stuart kings. They were friendly with France, England's old enemy.

Edinburgh

The Lowlands

The Border – Scots and English raided each other, stole cattle, and murdered whenever they could.

Flodden ✗
Solway Moss ✗

Henry VIII wanted to conquer Scotland.

Henry VIII went north once in 1540 after the rebellion, the Pilgrimage of Grace, 1537.

IRELAND

Ulster

English Kings were 'Lords of Ireland' until 1541.

The Pale in 1530, under English control

Dublin

Leinster

Munster

'More than sixty countries called regions inhabited with the King's Irish enemies were reigneth more than sixty chief captains that liveth by the sword and maketh war and peace for himself without any licence of the King.'
A report on Ireland by an official of Henry VIII, 1515

1534 – Several Irish chieftains rebelled.
1541 – Henry VIII made himself King of Ireland. All Irish land now belonged to him, and Irish chiefs held it with his permission.

WALES — Conquered by the English by 1295. Some English counties created then.

He never went to Wales or the West.

'I beg you to send down to us some man to use the sword of justice, otherwise the Welsh will war so wild it will not be easy to bring them to order again.'
An official on the border with Wales, writing to Henry VIII, 1534

1536 – The Act of Union, a law made by Parliament in England. Wales was divided into 13 counties, organised like English ones. Law courts and the King's officials all had to use English, not Welsh.

London ♛

Deptford – Royal dockyards for shipbuilding

The King spent most time in his 55 palaces in or near London.

PARLIAMENT	THE KING'S POWER – THE GOVERNMENT	THE RULING CLASSES
House of Lords — Nobles, Bishops, Judges **House of Commons** — Mostly gentry, Some merchants • agreed to any extra taxes the King needed (he was supposed to manage without) • made laws called Acts of Parliament, on the King's orders • gave advice – if asked	**Henry VIII** • made all important decisions • chose his ministers and his Council • got rid of them when he chose • decided when to call Parliament **But** • he spent more money than he had, so he could not afford an army, nor many royal officials outside London	Nobles and gentry in their home areas: • collected taxes • equipped and trained soldiers for the King • maintained law and order • looked after the poor • controlled wages • looked after roads and bridges

---

1.1 Do you think the writer of Source 1A is being flattering or truthful? Explain your opinion. *AT 3.3*

1.2 Why was Henry VIII so popular with most of his subjects when he became king? *AT 2.7*

1.3 Source 1B should remind you how jousting worked. What information about the sport can you find there?
Why was it still a popular sport for a king like Henry VIII, and his nobles? *AT 3.3 / AT 1.3*

The power of Henry VIII in Britain

Look carefully at the information on the map above.

1.4 What reasons can you find to explain why powerful kings like Henry VIII still needed to get on well with the ruling classes? *AT 1.3*

1.5 Why was Parliament important, although it only met when the King decided? *AT 1.3*

11

A WIDER WORLD

The four nations in Britain

The English, Welsh, Scots and Irish were independent peoples, each with their own culture, language and history. England was the richest, largest and strongest of the four nations. But Wales, Ireland and Scotland could cause her trouble because they were like three back doors which the English could never quite manage to keep securely locked. The map ◁11 shows how Henry VIII tried to do this – but he was not always successful.

Wales: Many Welsh landowners spoke English, and wanted to do well in England. They were pleased with the Act of Union. The Tudor family came from Wales, and some Welshmen already had jobs at court. Now they could be Members of Parliament as well. But most ordinary people only spoke Welsh, and never left Wales. The Act was hard on them.

In **Ireland,** it seemed at first to make little difference when Henry made himself their king, but English hold on Irish land would soon matter a great deal. Ireland remained a problem.

1.6 A modern Welsh historian said that the Act of Union drove the Welsh language into the kitchen. What did he mean?

AT 2

James IV of Scotland (1488–1513)

James IV became King of Scotland when he was only 16, during a rebellion against his father. He kept his powerful nobles in control, and the country peaceful. In his reign, Aberdeen University was founded, and the first Scots printers began work in Edinburgh. ◁9

Henry VII hoped that James IV's marriage with his daughter Margaret would bring lasting peace between England and Scotland. In this picture of 1600, James holds the flag of the red lion of Scotland, and Margaret's skirt is decorated with the English royal coat-of-arms 80▷. This marriage certainly linked England and Scotland closely, but not very peacefully

SOURCE 1C

Some items from James IV's accounts

Payments:
- to the Church and the shrines the King visited on pilgrimage
- to a poor man he saw by the roadside with a dead horse, and for a surgeon to treat a sailor who fell from the rigging of one of his ships
- to poets, musicians, and jugglers at court
- for jousting, including a three-day joust when James was champion for a 'black lady'
- to John Damian, an Italian who believed he could make a potion to give everlasting life. The King paid for a lot of whisky for him, and perhaps he was drunk when he tried to fly from the walls of Stirling Castle to Paris, with wings made of feathers – he fell straight into a dungheap.

The most payments were for:
- building Holyrood Palace, and a new chapel and great hall at Stirling Castle
- building ships, including £30,000 (a year's income) for the biggest one, *The Great Michael*. Henry VIII copied the design
- many different guns, with gunners to maintain them and transport them where they were needed.

THE PEOPLE OF BRITAIN

The Battle of Flodden

Henry VIII wanted glorious victories, and in 1513, he went to war with France, England's old enemy. James IV saw his chance to be a warrior king as well, and cause trouble for Henry. He sent his great warships to sea, and led his army (including the huge 'Mons Meg') over the border into England. But at Flodden, an English army cut the Scots to pieces. Probably 10,000 Scots soldiers were killed. The town of Selkirk sent a company of spearmen, and only one returned. Three bishops, 11 earls and 15 lords died. James's dead body was found under a heap of corpses.

The Battle of Flodden was a disaster for Scotland. James left a baby son, James V, and his widow Margaret Tudor had to try to rule the country for him. The marriage had not brought peace for long.

Later in his reign, Henry VIII decided to try to conquer Scotland. In 1542, the Scots were defeated again at Solway Moss. James V was already ill, and died soon after he heard the news. His baby daughter Mary, only six days old, became Queen. English armies burnt the city of Edinburgh, and stayed on Scots soil for several years. But the Scots were stronger than they seemed, and Henry VIII never became King of Scotland.

An Early Modern supergun – James IV's 'Mons Meg', the largest cannon in Britain, made in 1450. It is still in Edinburgh Castle

1.7 What does Source 1C tell you about James IV's character? Do you think he was like Henry VIII? *[AT 3.5]*

1.8 In pairs, work out what a Scots and English noble might think of each other by 1542. *[AT 1.6]*

A WIDER WORLD

Knowing your place

The inhabitants of the village of Bermondsey are having a good time in this picture. The fiddlers are playing away for the dancers in the centre, and the busy servants are bringing in huge pies. Some important looking people are coming out of the churchyard. They are the gentry; they own most of the land in the village, and the villagers depend on them for their jobs and their homes. Some rich and gaily dressed visitors are arriving on horseback on the left. They may be courtiers from one of the royal palaces. London is not far away – the River Thames and the Tower are in the distance.

The people in this picture of Tudor England accepted that they were born into different classes in society, and probably did not think about whether this was good or bad. But that did not stop them trying to do better for themselves, and going up in the world if they could.

SOURCE 1D A village party at Bermondsey, painted by Joris Hoefnagel in about 1571, during the reign of Elizabeth I

1.9 Use the people in Source 1D to make a list of the different classes in England, in order of importance. Look at page 11 and list the ways in which the people at the top controlled the lives of the rest.

AT 3.3

THE PEOPLE OF BRITAIN

Women's lives

The fine gentleman at the party in the foreground, wearing a hat and sweeping cloak, with his dog nearby, may have just got married. His wife is dressed in black, and is probably a widow, and mother of the three children (one a baby) just behind her. She may be more independent than most women in the Early Modern Age. A girl was under the control of her father until she married, and then she was supposed to obey her husband. But if he died, and he was rich enough to leave her land and goods, she could run his business or farm, and choose whether to marry again.

Women in the Early Modern Age worked hard. The wife of a noble had many servants, but also a huge household of perhaps 200 people to manage. A more ordinary country woman never seemed to stop:

SOURCE 1F

And when thou art up and ready, first sweep thy house, and set all things in good order; milk thy cows, strain the milk, take up thy children and dress them, and provide for thy husband's breakfast, dinner and supper, and for thy children and servants; take corn and malt to the mill to bake and brew ... make butter and cheese ... look after thy hens, ducks and geese ... make thy garden to get as many good seeds and herbs good for the pot ... grow flax for sheets, towels and other necessaries ... have your distaff ▷80◁ ready that thou be not idle ... go to market ... help thy husband fill the muck-cart, drive the plough, or load hay.

Some advice for farmers' wives, from Fitzherbert's *Book of Husbandry* (farming), 1523

SOURCE 1E
A scene just after the birth of a baby. At this time, many mothers and babies died during childbirth. Parents often lost half the children born to them, and at least one in every seven babies died before they were one – more in high risk areas like crowded towns

1.10 In Source 1E, say what all the people in the picture are doing. What evidence is there to explain why mothers and babies were more at risk in the sixteenth century than they are now? *AT 3.5*

1.11 How can you tell that Source 1F was written for people who were fairly well-off, but not 'gentry'? *AT 3.3*

1.12 Make a list of the things this housewife has to produce that today she could buy in shops. Then make a timetable of her work for a typical summer day.

As well as their tasks at home, women worked in the fields with the men, especially at busy times like hay-making (though two people here are not doing much work)

A WIDER WORLD

People and change

For ordinary people in country and town, houses, food, tools, and work had changed little for centuries. However, one change had already been going on in parts of England, especially the Midlands.

SOURCE 1G   At least six people were needed for every plough used to grow corn for food. But one shepherd could look after a great many sheep, and landowners made good profits selling fleeces to merchants trading in wool and cloth – England's main industry

Enclosures: In 1512, John Spencer, a sheep farmer, was given permission by the King to enclose land in Althorp, Northamptonshire, which meant he could put up fences on land being used by villagers for their crops, to keep in his sheep. A government inquiry in 1517 into enclosures mentioned him:

SOURCE 1H

He converted lands from their original cultivation into pasture for sheep, whereby four persons were made idle who up to then had been working there, to their great loss were driven to become wandering beggars.

We do not know what happened to the four beggars, but John Spencer became High Sheriff of Northamptonshire, and the Spencer family still own a beautiful house at Althorp.

1.13 Remind yourself how people lived and worked in medieval villages. Then use Sources 1G and 1H to explain what enclosures were, and the results they might have. What might **a** landowners and **b** villagers feel about them? [AT 3.5 / AT 1.6]

Population: The Black Death (1348–9) probably killed off about a third of all the people in Britain and Europe. The population did not increase again until the sixteenth century. There was no government census every ten years to count the population as there is now, but the facts in the table opposite have given historians clues.

1.14 The possible causes in the table opposite do not match the facts. Which possible causes do you think explain the facts? For example, does Cause 3 or 4 explain Fact A? Pair the letters and numbers to make a sensible cause explain a fact; think of other causes if you can; pool your results with the class. [AT 1.5]

SOURCE 1I   The skeleton Death snatches a child from his terrified family. Death was part of people's everyday lives, especially when food was short after a bad harvest, and in killer epidemics ▷80◁ of plague ▷80◁, typhus ▷80◁ and the 'sweating sickness', a dangerous type of 'flu. There were very few hospitals, only the rich could afford doctors, and cures were a matter of luck, because nobody yet understood the causes of most diseases

1.15 In Source 1I, what is the skeleton holding and why? How does the artist show this is a very poor family? [AT 3.3]

1.16 What evidence can you find on pages 14–17 that life was very hard for the poor in Tudor England? (There is more about this later.) [AT 1.4]

THE PEOPLE OF BRITAIN

	Fact		Possible cause
A	Prices were rising, especially food.	1	People tried to find work in towns, especially London.
B	Wages did not go up.	2	Printing spread information, and people were more aware of what was happening.
C	There seemed to be more poverty and unemployment.	3	Food was often scarce, especially when there were bad harvests.
D	There was much buying and selling of land, and rents went up.	4	There were not enough jobs to go round.
E	London's population 1500: 60,000 1600: 200,000	5	Too many people wanted land.

People in towns

Although nine out of every ten people still lived in the country in Tudor England, many towns were growing, especially London. See what you can find out about conditions in towns in Source 1J.

1.17 Take each regulation in Source 1J in turn and say what it tells you about Tudor York. [AT 3.5]

SOURCE 1J

No manner of person shall cast any filth of pigs or dogs against Greyfriars Wall.
No man dwelling on the banks of the Ouse shall cast any manner of filth into the said water of the Ouse.
Every alderman ▷80 of the city shall hang a lantern with a light burning over their door every night from five of the clock till nine.
Three corn merchants to see to the Town walls, to be kept clean, without weeds growing in the same, and to repair as much of the said walls now fallen.
All strange beggars [i.e. who do not live there] now being within this city to the common nuisance, shall leave this city within 24 hours, on pain of whipping of their bodies.

York City Council regulations, 1517–30

Trades in Towns: People lived in towns because they worked in trades being carried on there, or they went to towns hoping to find work. Trades were still organised into guilds, which made sure goods were properly produced, trained apprentices ▷80, and helped and entertained their members. But the growing population made things much more difficult. It was very hard for apprentices and journeymen (wage-earners) to set up on their own and become master tradesmen. If there was trouble in towns, disgruntled young workers often began it.

1.18 In Source 1K, what is everyone in the picture doing? What does it tell you about shops in Tudor towns? [AT 3.3]

1.19 What problems might there be between the master shoemaker and his workers? [AT 1.6]

SOURCE 1K

In this picture of a Tudor shoemaker's shop, find the master shoemaker, his wife and children, a journeyman and an apprentice who live with the family, and the customers

2 Church and people

The King's 'Great Matter'

Henry VIII considered himself a religious man [10]. In 1521, he even wrote a book defending the Pope, who rewarded him with a new title: Defender of the Faith. The letters FD on our modern coins stand for this.

Henry also usually got his own way, except for one thing – a son to rule after him. By 1527, after a marriage of nearly 20 years, he and Catherine of Aragon had one daughter, Mary, aged eleven – several baby sons had died. People took it for granted that women could not rule successfully. No woman had a chance to show they might be wrong, for a queen had not ruled England since Norman times.

Catherine had first been married to Henry's brother Arthur, who died soon after the wedding. Henry conveniently decided that he should never have married his brother's widow, and that he must have a divorce – which could only be granted by the Pope. Henry could think of little else. The divorce was his 'Great Matter'.

Catherine of Aragon was a sensible strong-minded woman who was much respected, and very religious. Her head-dress (a Spanish hood) had been fashionable when she was young. She was now middle-aged, and not likely to have more children. She had one advantage: her nephew, the Emperor Charles V [8] was the most powerful ruler in Europe. In 1527 he was not friendly to Henry VIII, and he had just taken the Pope prisoner

Anne Boleyn was a lady at court, and 20 years younger than Catherine. She was lively, clever and fashionable, with a sharp tongue. Though she was not beautiful, she knew how to make the best of her glossy dark hair and large eyes, and her head-dress (a French hood) was the latest fashion. Henry was deeply in love with her. She was determined to be queen, not just Henry's mistress

INVESTIGATION

How did changes in the Church affect people in Britain?

Key Sources
- Portraits by Holbein
- Foxe's *Book of Martyrs*
- Letters from the Spanish ambassador
- Acts of Parliament

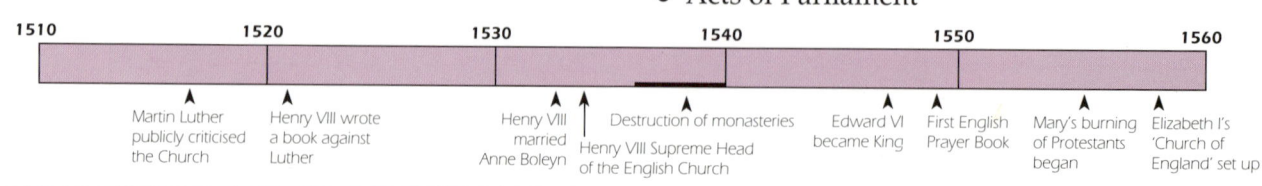

1510	1520	1530		1540	1550	1560
	Martin Luther publicly criticised the Church	Henry VIII wrote a book against Luther	Henry VIII married Anne Boleyn / Henry VIII Supreme Head of the English Church	Destruction of monasteries	Edward VI became King	First English Prayer Book	Mary's burning of Protestants began	Elizabeth I's 'Church of England' set up

CHURCH AND PEOPLE

> **SOURCE 2A**
>
> I put myself in great distress praying to you with all my heart that you will tell me of your whole mind concerning the love between us, having been now above one year struck with the dart of love.
>
> One of many letters from Henry to Anne, dated 1527. (Henry did not often write letters himself.)

> **SOURCE 2B**
>
> Sir, I beseech you, for all the love that hath been between us, let me have justice and right … I take God and all the world to witness that … this twenty years I have been your true wife.
>
> Catherine's speech to Henry at a court held at Blackfriars in 1529, on the Pope's orders. He did not grant the divorce.

2.1 What can you learn from Sources 2A and 2B, and the information above about how Henry, Catherine and Anne felt about the divorce?

AT 3.5 1.6

Servants of the King – Three men called Thomas

Thomas Wolsey was the son of a butcher. He rose to be Henry's Chancellor, and Archbishop of York. He held so many important church posts he was richer than the nobles at court, which made many of them jealous. Wolsey did not have time to do his work for the Church properly, but he served the King loyally, and loved grandeur as much as Henry did. He built the great palace of Hampton Court, and organised the 'Field of the Cloth of Gold' ◁2▷.

But the Pope was still in the power of the Emperor Charles V, Catherine's nephew, and Wolsey could not persuade him to grant the divorce. Henry was hard on people who failed him. Wolsey would have been executed for treason ◁80▷, if he had not died on his way to his trial in 1530.

Thomas Cranmer was a quiet scholar, interested in reforming the Church. He probably would have preferred to spend his life studying. He was a chaplain to Anne Boleyn, and Henry made him his Archbishop of Canterbury in 1532. In 1533 he held a special court in England which gave Henry his divorce at last, without asking the Pope. Just before that, Henry secretly married Anne. She was pregnant, and of course the baby would be a son. But in September 1533, Anne had a baby girl, Elizabeth. Henry was bitterly disappointed, and maybe already his feelings towards Anne began to change.

Thomas Cromwell was a clever, efficient man, who had been a soldier, lawyer, merchant and Member of Parliament before he became the King's chief minister in 1532. He helped Henry to find a different way to get his divorce. Why bother about the Pope or the Emperor? English churchmen should obey the King, not the Pope, like all his other subjects. Cromwell made careful plans for Parliament to make laws which gave the King new powers over the Church, while Cranmer gave the King his divorce.

In 1534, Parliament passed a new law, which made Henry Supreme Head of the Church in England. Soon all important people had to swear they accepted Anne Boleyn as queen. There would be trouble if they refused.

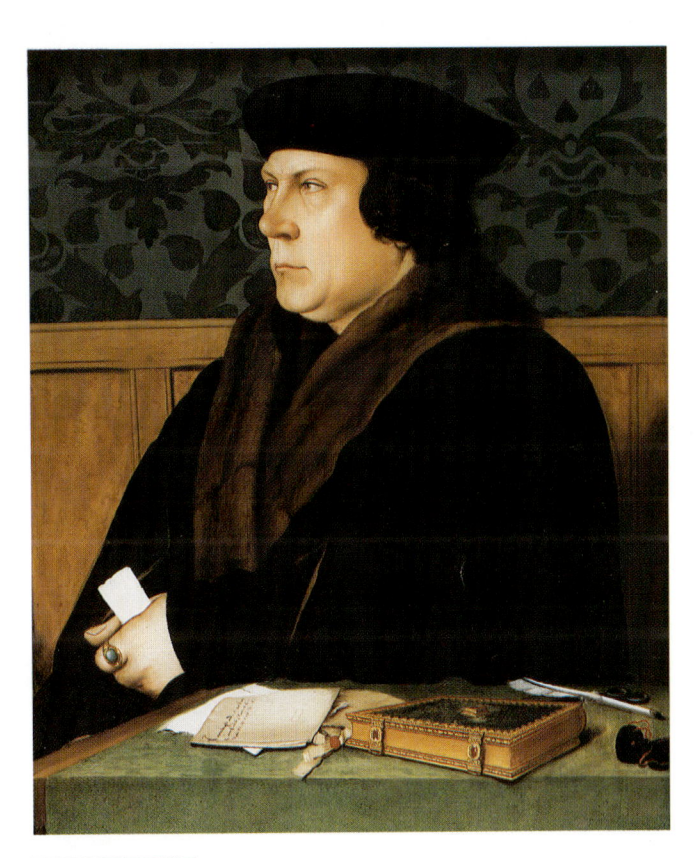

SOURCE 2C A good copy of a portrait by the great artist Holbein ◁4▷. Cromwell wears black – not coloured silk or velvet like a nobleman – and his writing materials are on the desk in front of him

2.2 In Source 2C, how has Holbein shown what kind of person Cromwell is?

AT 3.3

2.3 Make a strip cartoon of the main events in the story of Henry VIII's divorce from 1527 to 1534. Underneath, explain why Henry made himself Supreme Head of the Church, and why Parliament is important in the story.

AT 1.4

19

A WIDER WORLD

The Reformation in Europe

While Henry VIII was taking over the English Church because he wanted a divorce, a much bigger religious revolution, called the Reformation, was going on in Europe. This page shows how the Reformation split up the Christian Church. The rest of the chapter investigates how the Reformation affected the people of Britain.

The great church of St Peter in Rome. Its rebuilding began in 1506. The design of this impressive Renaissance church was based on the temples of ancient Greece and Rome ◁8. The Romans discovered how to construct a dome, and their skill was copied in the Renaissance. The artist Michelangelo helped to design this dome.

The centre of the Catholic Church – in 1500 the largest organisation in Europe. Everyone in western Europe (often then called Christendom) was a member of the one Catholic Church, headed by the Pope in Rome. They attended the same Latin services in the same kind of church buildings.

Trouble over the rebuilding. The Pope wanted St Peter's to impress everyone with the power of the Church – this huge and beautiful building would help people to worship God. But many people thought St Peter's cost too much, and that the Pope and other leading churchmen were much too interested in wealth and power.

Scholars challenged the Church's teaching. They said that relics 80▷, pictures and statues in churches were treated like magic charms, and made people superstitious 80▷. The famous scholar Erasmus once said there were enough pieces of wood from the 'true' cross of Jesus to build a ship.

The Latin translation of the Bible used by the Church had too many mistakes. Martin Luther and other reformers taught that people should be able to read the Bible in their own language, without the help of priests. Then they could learn God's word, put their faith in Christ, and win a place in Heaven.

Martin Luther first broke away from the Catholic church in Germany in 1521. He and his followers were called **Protestants** because they protested against the Catholic Church. Protestants did not always agree with each other. Jean Calvin founded a separate Protestant Church in Geneva from 1536.

Divided Christians

	Catholics	Protestants
Church services	In Latin. The priest, wearing special clothes called vestments, stood apart from the people at the altar, with a cross and candles on it. Pictures and statues were used to help people to worship God, and teach them the beliefs of the Church. A relic often had an important place in the church. Big churches had fine music and organs.	In the people's own language. The minister wore a plain black gown, and sometimes a white tunic called a surplice. He taught the Bible in long sermons. Instead of an altar there was a plain table. There were no pictures and statues, because Protestants believed they made people superstitious.
Organisation	The Pope in Rome, with archbishops and bishops, priests, monks and nuns. They were not allowed to marry.	No Pope, monks or nuns. Some Protestant churches kept bishops. Followers of Calvin chose their own ministers, and ran their own church's affairs. Priests or ministers could marry.

CHURCH AND PEOPLE

A Bible people could understand

In 1539, Henry allowed the first official Bible in English to be printed. Every church was ordered to buy one. This was a big step, because Protestants believed everyone should be able to read the Bible in their own language. But Henry was not a Protestant – he wanted to run the English Church instead of the Pope. So he made sure everyone realised he was in control when they opened the first page.

Henry soon had second thoughts about allowing everyone to read the Bible. He ordered Parliament to pass a law forbidding 'Women, apprentices, serving men and labourers' to read it, because 'It was disputed, rhymed, sung and jangled in every alehouse'. But it was too late. People went on reading the English Bible, and it became one of the most important books in the English language.

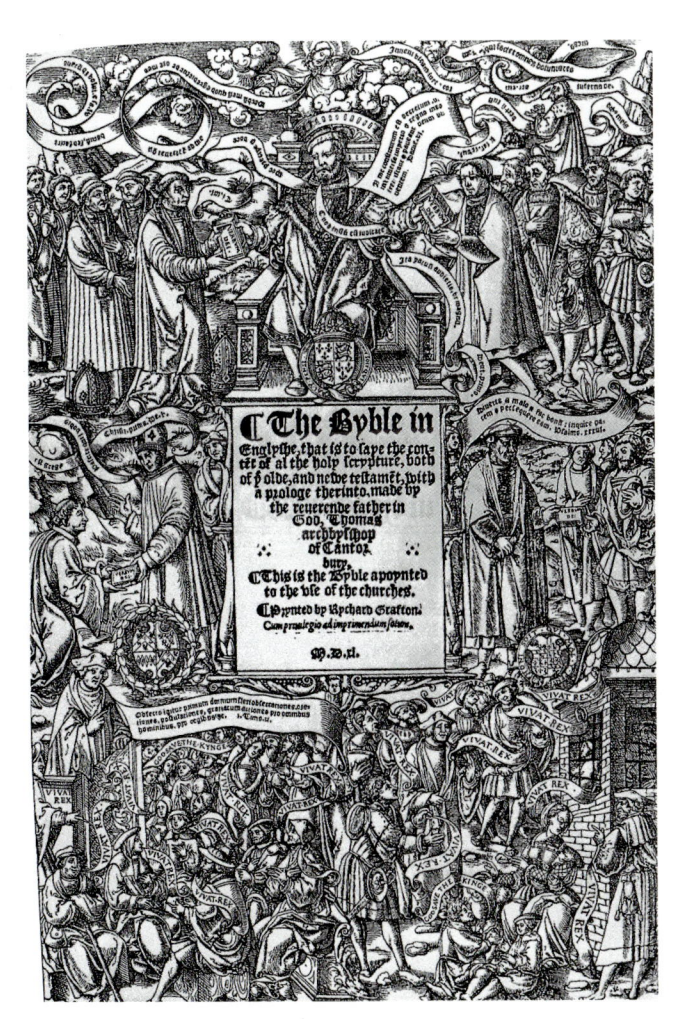

The first page of the English Bible. Henry VIII hands out the Bible to his bishops and nobles, and the ordinary people below. God is above the King, blessing him – but who looks the most important in the picture?

The Bible in Welsh

William Morgan was a Welsh parish priest in Denbighshire in the 1580s. By that time services had to be in English, but William was worried because his Welsh-speaking villagers could not understand what was going on. He said they came:

> eagerly into the church to hear the sermon, listened carefully, yet went away confused and muddled, like men who had found a rich treasure which they could not dig out, or who had gone to a banquet and were not allowed to eat.

So, as well as serving his parish, he began to translate the whole Bible into Welsh, writing by hand with a quill pen – no typewriters or word processors then. But William stuck to his task, and it took him six years. When it was finished at last, the Welsh Bible was printed in London, by English printers who did not know Welsh, so William had to spend a year in London, checking every word.

The first Bible in Welsh was published in 1588. It was easy to understand and interesting to listen to. It helped to keep the Welsh language lively and popular. A Welsh poet, Ieuan Tew, wrote: 'The great Bible in our tongue is the sun that gives light.'

2.4 Choose from the phrases like **this** to complete this sentence sensibly, and explain your choice: *AT 1.5*

Henry VIII's law about Bible reading shows that:

only rich men/some ordinary men and women could read by now.

printed books were **expensive/reasonably cheap**.

Henry was **worried/not worried** that Bible reading might encourage ordinary people to think for themselves, and cause trouble.

2.5 Why do laws telling people what they are allowed to read usually not work? *AT 1.3*

2.6 Why was the Welsh language supposed to be used less after 1536? ◁11 How did the Welsh Bible help to keep it alive? *AT 1.4*

A WIDER WORLD

The end of the monasteries

Nuns singing one of the eight services they had to attend every 24 hours. The three big knots in their girdles were there to remind them of the three vows all monks and nuns made – to give up their possessions, to give up sexual relations, and to obey their superiors

When Henry VIII made himself Supreme Head of the Church in England in 1534, he still had not touched a very big part of the Church – over 800 monasteries and nunneries. Many of them were rich. They owned about a quarter of the land in England, gold and silver treasures, and beautiful handwritten books. Some had famous shrines, like the tomb of Thomas Becket in Canterbury, and made money from pilgrims who came to worship there.

Henry VIII decided to destroy the monasteries for two reasons:

- monks and nuns might obey the Pope and not him
- he was short of money.

But he had to be careful how he did it. Monasteries and nunneries had been part of local communities for centuries. The local village priest often came from the nearby monastery. Monks and nuns sometimes provided hospitality for travellers, cared for the sick and the poor, or ran schools. They did not always do these jobs well, but few other people looked after these important needs.

Thomas Cromwell's investigation

Henry ordered his minister Thomas Cromwell to organise the destruction of the monasteries. First Cromwell needed to 'prove' that monks and nuns were not doing their job properly. In 1535, he sent officials with a list of questions to all monasteries – and expected the right kind of answers.

Questions and answers

Some questions asked by Cromwell's men: How many church services do you attend daily? What food do you eat? Do you leave the monastery? Can you read and write?

SOURCE 2D

As for the abbot, we found nothing suspect about his living, except he spent much time in his granges [houses belonging to the abbot some distance from the monastery], that he delighted much in playing at die and cards and therein spent much money ... there was here more women coming and going than any other monastery. Amongst the relics we found ... the coals that St Lawrence was toasted with, the paring of St Edmund's nails, and magic charms to cure headaches.

Report on the abbey of Bury St Edmund's, Suffolk

2.7 What other questions must Cromwell's officials have asked at Bury St Edmunds Abbey? [AT 3.3]

2.8 Remember what you learnt about monasteries in the Middle Ages. What were Cromwell's officials trying to find out? [AT 1.2]

2.9 Is Source 2D evidence of what all monasteries were like in 1535? Explain your answer carefully. [AT 2.4 3.7]

CHURCH AND PEOPLE

[Photograph of Fountains Abbey ruins with labels:]
- Bells from the tower
- Treasures from the church
- Lead from the roof
- Stones from the walls – some was used in Fountains Hall, built nearby in 1598
- Land – sold by the King to a merchant, Sir Richard Gresham

SOURCE 2E A modern photograph of the ruins of Fountains Abbey in Yorkshire

The destruction

Cromwell's investigation found plenty wrong with monasteries, and some of it was true. The King had what he wanted – the excuse to destroy the monasteries. In 1536, he ordered Parliament to pass an Act closing down the small monasteries. Three years later, even the largest were empty. The King took land and everything valuable – books, gold and jewels, bells, and building materials, especially lead. Three abbots who held out against the King, from Reading, Colchester and Glastonbury, were hanged, but many others got good jobs and pensions. Monks and nuns were given pensions and went quietly. Many monks became parish priests, but nuns had a harder time. Their pensions were smaller, and Henry VIII forbade them to marry – but what else could they do?

Cromwell hoped the King would keep the land, and make money from renting it out. But Henry went on spending a great deal, especially as he went to war again in 1542 ◀4. By the end of his reign he had sold most of the monastery lands to his nobles and other landowners. They did well out of the monasteries, and did not want to see them come back.

What happened at Hailes Abbey, Gloucestershire

- The abbot had a pension of £100 a year.
- Monks had on average £5 a year – 16 out of 20 became parish priests.
- The King took: lead from the roof, bells, gold and silver treasure.
- The monastery's famous relic, the 'Holy Blood' was declared to be 'honey clarified and coloured with saffron, as has been evidently proved before the King and his council'.
- The land was bought and sold several times, mainly by local landowners.
- Local people took stone, window frames, iron bars, locks and keys – anything useful for building.
- There is just a ruin there now.

2.10 Make a list of the labels in Source 2E, and say what happened to each. (Guess sensibly if you need to.) — AT 3.5

2.11 Do you think there would have been much opposition to the closing of Hailes Abbey? Explain your answer carefully. — AT 1.5

2.12 In groups, work out and act two scenes: Cromwell's men interviewing monks and local people; the closing down of a monastery/nunnery. — AT 1.6

A WIDER WORLD

Challenges to Henry VIII

Most of Henry VIII's subjects accepted Henry as Supreme Head of the English Church. A few were brave enough to say he was wrong.

Sir Thomas More (1476–1535) was a clever scholar and lawyer. He wrote a best-selling book called *Utopia* about an imaginary island where everyone shared their money, possessions and work – he was criticising wealth and selfishness, especially in the Church. Thomas was very religious, and nearly became a monk as a young man. At first, Henry VIII admired him, and when Wolsey failed to get Henry his divorce in 1529, Henry made Thomas his Chancellor. But Thomas disapproved of the divorce, and the King's break with the Pope. Soon he resigned, and refused to swear the oath accepting Anne Boleyn as Queen ◀19.

The King tried to force Thomas to change his mind. He was imprisoned in a small damp cell in the Tower. His family were forced to go and plead with him to give in. He was questioned many times, and his books were taken away. For 17 months, Thomas More remained silent. In the end, he was put on trial and executed. On the scaffold he said: 'I die the King's good servant, but God's servant first.'

SOURCE 2F The family of Sir Thomas More – a drawing by Holbein in 1527. It is an unusual picture because no one is posing for the artist. They are getting ready for family prayers, and the room is rather untidy.

Find: Sir Thomas More – the chain round his neck shows he is an important adviser to the King; his father and son; his wife kneeling at a desk, with a pet monkey in her skirts; five daughters (two are adopted); a servant standing by the door

2.13 Why did Henry VIII make Thomas More his Chancellor, and then turn against him? Why did Thomas hold out against the King?

2.14 Make a strip cartoon of the life and death of Thomas More.

2.15 Use Source 2F to make labelled sketches of costumes and a wealthy family's room in the 1520s.

AT 1.6

AT 3.3

The Pilgrimage of Grace was a serious rebellion in 1537 in the north of England, led by Robert Aske, a strong Catholic. Henry crushed it ruthlessly. One hundred and seventy-eight people were executed; Robert Aske was hung in chains from the walls of York Castle and left to die. There was no more trouble in the north for a time, but many people there stayed loyal to the Catholic Church.

> SOURCE 2G
>
> To have the supreme head of the Church restored to Rome.
> To have the abbeys restored to their lands and goods.
> To punish the lord Cromwell, who destroys the good laws of this realm, and encourages heretics.
> To enforce the law against enclosures [16].
> To be permitted not to pay taxes now agreed by Parliament.
> To have Parliament in Nottingham or York.
>
> Some of the demands made to Henry VIII by the leaders of the Pilgrimage of Grace, 1537

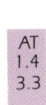

The old Henry VIII. He had a bad ulcer on his leg, which (it was said) sometimes made him go black in the face with agony, and he was so overweight that a special machine hauled him up and downstairs. Compare this picture with the one on page 4

2.16 Was the Pilgrimage of Grace a rebellion about religion? Use Source 2G to decide what the rebels felt strongly about.

Henry VIII and his wives

Catherine of Aragon was banished from court in 1531, and never saw her daughter Mary again. She died in 1536. [20]

Anne Boleyn had another child after Elizabeth – a son, born dead. Henry was already tired of her sharp tongue, and accused her of having a lover, though she was probably too realistic to do anything so risky. She was beheaded in 1536 with a sword, not an axe, as a sign of 'mercy'.

Jane Seymour was one of Anne's ladies at court, a quiet girl who came from a Protestant family. Henry married her 11 days after Anne's execution. Jane had the son Henry had wanted for so long – Edward, born 1537. But she died 12 days later.

Anne of Cleves was a German princess. In 1540, Cromwell persuaded Henry to ally with some German Protestant princes, including Anne's father. Henry was not keen – even less keen when he saw Anne. He apparently said she looked like a horse, and divorced her straight away. It was the end of Cromwell too; he was executed soon after.

Catherine Howard was a young pretty niece of the Duke of Norfolk, one of Henry's most powerful nobles, who disliked Protestants. Henry married her in 1540, as soon as his divorce was rushed through. He was unhealthy and overweight by now. Catherine had a lover, and Henry found out. In 1542, she was executed.

Katherine Parr was a sensible widow, who may have been Protestant. Henry married her in 1543, and she looked after him and his three children. The King died in 1547, and Katherine survived him.

2.16 Make a chart of Henry's wives, with columns headed: **Name of wife, Date of marriage, Children, What happened to her.**

2.17 Divide into groups, and think of questions you would like to ask Henry VIII if you could – about what he believed and the reasons for his actions. Then work out the answers you think he might give, and choose actors to perform the interviews.

A WIDER WORLD

Protestant king and Catholic queen

SOURCE 2H

A picture painted by order of Edward VI's council in 1549. Henry VIII on his deathbed passes on his power to Edward VI aged 9.

Thomas Cranmer, the Protestant Archbishop of Canterbury [21] is amongst Edward's councillors, third from left. He wrote the English Prayer Book which had to be used in all churches by Act of Parliament.

The English Bible at Edward's feet crushes the Pope, and two monks run away. Soldiers pull down a Catholic statue of the Virgin Mary and burn pictures and carvings taken from churches (top right)

A queen to rule

In spite of everything Henry did to make sure he had a son to rule after him, in 1553 a queen ruled England for the first time for 400 years.

Edward died of tuberculosis when he was 16. The dying boy king and some of his councillors wanted a Protestant to follow him. They chose a queen they thought they could easily control – Edward's 16-year-old Protestant cousin Lady Jane Grey [79]. But most people wanted the rightful Queen – Henry VIII's eldest daughter, the Catholic Mary [79]. Jane, who never wanted to be Queen, ruled for only nine days, and was executed a year later.

2.18 Explain why Source 2H is a made up scene, which could not possibly have happened like this. *AT 3.7*

2.19 Explain what ideas the picture wants you to believe, and what evidence it gives about Edward VI's reign. *AT 3.5*

2.20 Why did people dread a minority, when a child was on the throne? *AT 1.6*

2.21 Were there more problems over a marriage for a reigning queen in Tudor times, than for a king? If so, why? *AT 1.5*

A shilling coin of 1557, with the heads of Mary and Philip on it

Mary's aim – To make England Catholic again

Problem 1 Who to marry? An English noble? Other nobles would be jealous. A foreign prince? England would be tied to a foreign power.

Problem 2 An unpopular marriage with Philip of Spain, who was not interested in England and soon left. Mary desperately wanted a son, but her hopes were disappointed.

Problem 3 War and defeat. Spain was at war with France, and England was dragged in. Calais was lost – the last English possession in Europe. This was seen as a terrible disgrace.

Problem 4 Hard times. Bad harvests made food short; an epidemic of 'sweating sickness' [16] killed many people.

Problem 5 Changes in religion. Many people were glad to go back to the old ways, but the new owners of monastery lands did not give them up, and the burning of Protestants was not popular.

Problem 6 Lack of time. Mary's reign only lasted five years – not long enough to do all she wanted.

CHURCH AND PEOPLE

Heretics or martyrs

Like many religious people of her time, Mary believed she should punish 'heretics', and ordered her bishops to hunt out Protestants. Nearly 800 escaped to Protestant centres in Europe. About 270 people were burnt in England. They believed they were martyrs, dying for their beliefs, not heretics.

People were used to public executions then, but Mary's persecution was unpopular, perhaps because many ordinary people suffered. Philip of Spain was blamed (wrongly). The burnings were not forgotten either, partly because a Protestant exile, John Foxe, vividly described them in his *Book of Martyrs*, published in 1563 after Mary died. Foxe was not an eyewitness, but he knew people who were. He did not actually make things up, but his book is very biased, and full of gory details. It became a best-seller, and was often kept in churches.

SOURCE 2I Even those who could not read Foxe's 'Book of Martyrs' could look at the illustrations. This one shows the burning in Oxford of two famous Protestant bishops, Hugh Latimer and Nicholas Ridley. The old Archbishop Cranmer (top left) was forced to watch from his prison – his turn would soon come. When he faced burning, he gave up his Protestant faith for a time, but in the end died bravely

SOURCE 2J

Facts and figures

Places where Protestants were burnt: London: 46 • Middlesex: 13 • Essex: 52 • Kent: 59 • Sussex: 27 • Hertfordshire: 3 • East Anglia: 35 • Gloucestershire: 10 • Oxford: 3 • Midlands: 14 • Wales: 3 • Devon and Cornwall: 1 • the north of England: 1.

People burnt: mainly weavers, clothmakers and tradesmen, including over 50 women. Also 4 bishops and 16 priests.

SOURCE 2K

The people of this town of London are murmuring about the cruel enforcement of the recent Acts of Parliament on heresy ... when a certain Rogers was burnt yesterday. Some of the onlookers wept, others gathered ashes and bones and wrapped them in paper to preserve them, yet others threatening the bishops. The haste with which the bishops have proceeded in this matter may well cause a revolt. Your Majesty might inform the bishops there are other means of punishing the obstinate, such as secret executions, banishment and imprisonment.

The Spanish ambassador's report to Philip of Spain, 5 February 1555

SOURCE 2L

So John Rogers was brought to Smithfield, there to be burnt, where he showed the most constant patience, urging the people to remain in that faith he had taught. And there in the presence of a wonderful number of people, the fire was put to him; and when it had taken hold upon his legs and shoulders, he, as one feeling no pain, washed his hands in the flames as though it had been cold water. And after lifting his hands to Heaven, most mildly this happy martyr yielded up his spirit into the hands of his heavenly Father. His wife and children, being 11 in number and one sucking at the breast, met him by the way as he walked to Smithfield, but he constantly and cheerfully took his death in defence of Christ's gospel.

John Foxe's account of the death of John Rogers, published 1563

2.22 From Sources 2K and 2L, decide what are facts, and what are opinions. (Make lists.) How does Source 2L show bias?

2.23 Which source tells you most about the crowd, and which concentrates on John Rogers? Are there reasons for this? What might each source have left out?

2.24 Explain what both writers felt about the burning of Protestants.

2.25 Use sources and information to make a list of reasons why Mary's burnings were unpopular at the time, and later.

2.26 Use Source 2J. On an outline map of England, put labels of the places, with numbers of people burnt. Shade labels in three colours, with key, for: places with under 10 Protestants burnt; 10 to 20; 20 and over. Make a block graph from the figures. Then explain where there were most burnings (think of reasons if possible).

A WIDER WORLD

The middle way

Elizabeth I was given a great welcome when she rode into London as Queen after Mary's death in 1558. Like Mary she had a difficult childhood, with four stepmothers. In Mary's reign when it was dangerous not to go to Catholic services, Elizabeth usually found some excuse – she was often 'not well'. Most people, including Mary, thought she was Protestant, and she was imprisoned in the Tower for a time. She learnt to be cautious and hide her feelings.

> *She is much attached to her people, and is very confident they are on her side ... she seems to me more feared than her sister, and gives her orders and has her way as absolutely as her father did.*
>
> The Spanish ambassador to Philip of Spain, 1558

Elizabeth was determined to 'have her way' over religion, because there had been so many confusing changes. She wanted a 'middle way' between Catholic and Protestant – and no more changes. She was lucky. She reigned for 45 years, so people had time to get used to the Church of England, though some never accepted it.

Changes in the English Church

	Catholic		Protestant
Henry VIII 1509–47 (Jan.)		Henry Supreme Head / The end of the monasteries / The English Bible	
Edward VI Jan. 1547–July 1553			The English Prayer Book / No statues or pictures in churches
Mary I July 1553–Nov. 1558		The Pope's power restored / Protestants persecuted	
Elizabeth I Nov. 1558–March 1603	Many Catholics could not accept the new Church. They were fined 1s if they did not attend its services.	**The Church of England 1559** • Kept bishops and familiar church buildings • Prayer Book services based on Catholic ones • Queen Head of Church • No Pope, monks or nuns • Few pictures and statues in church • The English Bible • Prayer Book services in English • Clergy could marry	Some Protestants thought the Church should be much more Protestant. They were called Puritans.

◀ **Catholic altar**
1. The rood with statues of Jesus on the Cross, Mary and John
2. Rood screen in front of the altar
3. The priest wearing vestments
4. The altar
5. Latin Mass book
6. Stained glass window

Church of England communion table ▶
1. Words from the Bible painted on whitewashed walls
2. Minister wearing a white surplice over a black cassock
3. Communion table with bread and wine, and the English Prayer Book
4. Plain glass window

Catholic and Protestant Churches

CHURCH AND PEOPLE

Ordinary people and their parish church

Trouble in the south west

SOURCE 2M

We will not receive the new service because it is like a Christmas game, but we will have our old services in Latin, not in English. And so we the Cornishmen (some of us understand no English) utterly refuse this new English service.

One of the demands of rebels in Devon and Cornwall, 1549 ◁26

2.27 Which change do these people dislike? What can you learn about the people who wrote this demand? [AT 3.3]

2.28 Work in groups. Use page 20, the chart, 'Changes in the English Church', Source 2N and the pictures below. For each year, work out who was King or Queen, and what change was going on. Make sure you understand each item in the accounts. If time, make a picture of the church in 1555, and 1562. [AT 1.3]

Now your group becomes the church-wardens of St Giles's Church. Some of you are Protestants, some are Catholics, and some just want a quiet life. Each group should choose from accounts B–D. Argue for or against each item. Report back to the rest of the class. Discuss how people may have felt about these changes in their familiar parish church. [AT 1.6]

A town church in Reading, Berkshire

In every parish church, officials called church-wardens had to keep accounts of everything paid for, or received (for items sold), for each year. Here is a modernised version of some of the accounts of St Giles's Church, Reading:

SOURCE 2N

A March 1545 to March 1546

Received: for a candle for the rood light at Christmas	8s	3d
Paid: for cleaning the candlesticks		8d
for incense		7d
for making the candle for the rood, and Easter candles	17s	8d

B March 1548 to March 1551

Received: for gold or silver vessels used on the altar	4s	4d
Paid: for three books of psalms		16d
for painting the church white [this covered up wall paintings of Bible scenes or stories of the saints]		16d
Paid: for digging out the stone altars in the church and carrying away the rubble	8s	2d
for making a surplice [plain white tunic worn in church] for Mr Vicar		20d
1553: for making a table [instead of an altar]	3s	10d

C March 1553 to March 1554

Received for alabaster statues and banner poles [N.B. This receipt must have been before July 1553]	8s	8d
Paid: for 2 candlesticks, a censer [for incense], and a pyx [a special box to hold the bread used in the Mass 80▷]	5s	8d
for candles	17s	8d
for a Mass book		5d
for painting the rood		20d
for making a cross		20d
1555: for a vestment [worn in church by the priest]	26s	8d

D March 1559 to March 1560

Paid: for pulling down the images		4d
for a Bible		14d
for whitewash for the walls	6s	0d
for pulling down the altars and getting rid of rubbish	2s	8d
for a communion table	4s	0d
1562: paid for taking down the rood	3s	4d
Received for vestments	£8 10s	0d

3 Elizabeth I and her world

The Queen and her court

Make-up: a thick white paste made of powdered eggshells, egg-white, alum, borax and poppy seeds (A pale skin like the Queen's was fashionable.)

Double sleeves: padded with horsehair, separate from the dress, and pinned or tied with tapes

The farthingale: held out by a frame of metal or whalebone hoops and several underskirts

A red wig covered with pearls and other jewels hides grey hair

Two ruffs: stiffened with starch, first imported from Holland in 1564, making this fashion possible

The triangular stomacher (bodice) stiffened with whalebone: reaches below the real waist – where is that?

Pearls, sapphires, rubies and emeralds blaze on the hair and dress, even on the hem

SOURCE 3A Elizabeth I in 1592 when she was almost 60, painted by Marcus Gheeraedts

Elizabeth I's portraits were messages to her subjects that their Queen was powerful, successful, and would never grow old. In other words, they were propaganda. Elizabeth had smallpox when she was 29, and may have lost her hair then. She certainly wore a red wig and thick white make-up as she got older. She controlled her portraits closely, though other people usually had to pay for them.

INVESTIGATIONS

How did Elizabeth I solve the problems of a woman ruler?
Why did she face so many threats?

Key Sources:
- Portraits of famous Elizabethans
- Acts of Parliament
- Records of ministers and local officials

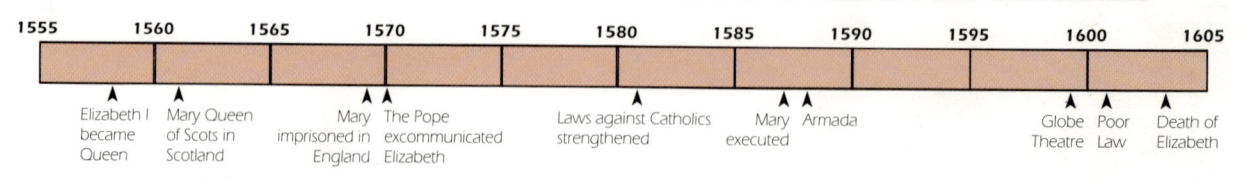

| 1555 | 1560 | 1565 | 1570 | 1575 | 1580 | 1585 | 1590 | 1595 | 1600 | 1605 |

- Elizabeth I became Queen
- Mary Queen of Scots in Scotland
- Mary imprisoned in England
- The Pope excommunicated Elizabeth
- Laws against Catholics strengthened
- Mary executed
- Armada
- Globe Theatre
- Poor Law
- Death of Elizabeth

ELIZABETH I AND HER WORLD

3.1 Work out the messages in Source 3A:
  a Why is the Queen wearing white?
  b What is the flower in her ruff?
  c What is she standing on? (Don't just look at her feet.)
  d Why is the sky painted like this?
  e Does the Queen look her age?

3.2 Sir Henry Lee, a courtier, ordered this picture to be painted. Why is his view of the Queen not very realistic?

AT 3.3

AT 2.5

The marriage game

Elizabeth I was a woman in a world of men. Everyone expected her to get married, just like her sister Mary ◁27◁. Philip II of Spain offered to marry her when she became Queen – 'to relieve her of those labours which are only fit for men'.

Elizabeth knew how much people disliked Mary's marriage. But at first, she needed Philip as a friend. So she pretended she was interested. Later other foreign princes suggested marriage. If Elizabeth wanted their country's friendship, she often seemed on the point of marrying, but she never did.

Many people thought Elizabeth would marry her favourite, the Earl of Leicester. He was a proud, rather unreliable man, and other courtiers distrusted him. Perhaps she realised the marriage would be a disaster, but although she was often angry with him (especially when he married someone else) he never lost her favour

Did Elizabeth really want to marry? She sometimes seemed to want it, but we do not know what she really felt. Some things she said are clues:

> SOURCE 3B
>
> *I have already joined myself to a husband, namely the Kingdom of England ... I will marry as soon as I conveniently can.*
>
> From a speech to Members of Parliament, when they asked her to marry in 1566
>
> *I will have here but one mistress and no master.*
>
> The Queen to the Earl of Leicester when he ordered about one of her servants

3.3 How does the Earl of Leicester's portrait tell you he is rich and important?

AT 3.3

3.4 Why do you think Elizabeth did not get married?

AT 1.4

Sunshine and storms

Elizabeth's courtiers were fond of flattering the Queen by saying that when she smiled it was like the sun shining, and when she was angry it was like a terrible storm (a clue about Source 3A). She liked to be called the 'Fairy Queen', even when she was a middle-aged woman wearing a wig and a lot of make-up. She gave her favourites nicknames. Leicester was her 'Eyes'. Her most trusted servant was William Cecil. She called him her 'Spirit'. When she became Queen she said to him:

> *This judgement I have of you that ... you will be faithful to the state, and that ... you will give me that counsel [advice] which you think best.*

The Queen was right about Cecil. He was sensible and practical, and served her faithfully until he died in 1598. During his last illness, the old Queen sat with him and fed him herself.

3.5 Write a paragraph describing Elizabeth's character, using the sources on this page.

AT 3.4

A WIDER WORLD

A queen in Scotland

Another Mary now comes into the story – the grandaughter of James IV [12]. Her father died when she was only a few days old, after Henry VIII's victory at Solway Moss. The English had a neat solution: Mary would marry Henry's son Edward, and Scotland would come under English rule at last. As you might expect, the Scots disliked that idea. Mary was sent to France, where she grew up and married the French King. She loved France and was very happy there.

Mary Queen of Scots. She was tall, slim and red-haired, and considered very beautiful when she was young. She was 36 and in prison when this portrait was painted

The Reformation in Scotland

Mary Queen of Scots was Catholic, and so was her mother, who ruled Scotland while Mary was in France. But Protestant teachings were spreading, especially in Edinburgh, and the Lowlands. The Scots already had the Bible in their own language (1543). At the beginning of Elizabeth's reign, the English helped the Scots Protestants, and although the Catholic government tried to stop it, a Protestant 'Kirk' (Church) was set up in 1560, which followed the teachings of Calvin [20]. Its followers were called **Presbyterians**.

John Knox was a fiery Protestant preacher who hated Catholics – and women rulers. He was the most important leader of the new Protestant 'Kirk'. Not surprisingly he did not get on with Mary when she returned to Scotland

The two queens

Just after Elizabeth I became Queen of England, Mary's husband, the French King, died suddenly. Mary, aged 19, sadly returned to rule the Scotland she did not know. Elizabeth and Mary were cousins [79]. They were rivals too, because:

- if Elizabeth had no children, Mary was her heir
- Elizabeth was Protestant, Mary was Catholic
- some English Catholics did not accept Elizabeth as Queen. They supported Mary.

ELIZABETH I AND HER WORLD

Marriages, murders and rebellion

Mary soon married again. Her new husband, Henry Darnley, was tall and handsome, but also weak, big-headed, and a drunkard. Mary soon became very unhappy, and spent a lot of time with her Italian secretary, David Riccio. Darnley was jealous. One evening, Darnley and other nobles burst into Mary's room in Holyrood Palace where she was having a supper party. Riccio clung terrified to the Queen's skirts. The nobles dragged him out of the room and stabbed him over 50 times.

Soon after, Mary gave birth to a son, James. She seemed to make it up with Darnley – but relied on a Protestant noble, the Earl of Bothwell.

On Sunday, 9 February 1567, Darnley was staying in a house called Kirk O'Field, in Edinburgh. He had been ill, and Mary was looking after him. Late in the evening, Mary left the house to join a wedding party. Darnley was in bed in an upstairs room. Suddenly there was a huge explosion, and the house blew up. The bodies of Darnley and his servant were found in the garden strangled. The explosion had not touched them. No one knows what really happened.

Three months later Mary married Bothwell (he had to divorce his wife first). Everyone thought he had murdered Darnley, but Mary did nothing about it. There was a rebellion, Mary was taken prisoner, and her baby son James 79▷ was made King. Bothwell escaped to Denmark, and died miserably in prison. Mary finally escaped too – over the border into England.

3.6 Write your own story of what might have happened at Kirk O'Field, explaining why the four labelled objects might be there. *AT 1.3*

3.7 Why were Mary's marriages to Darnley and Bothwell both disasters? *AT 1.5*

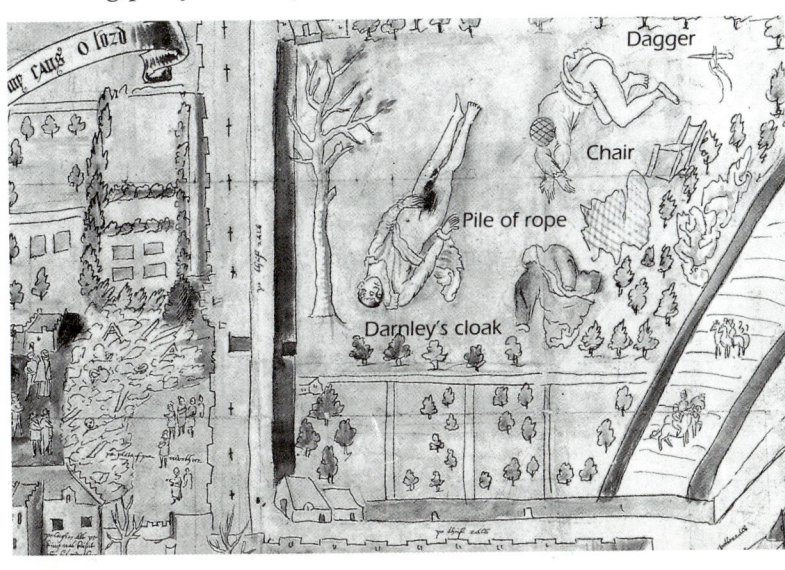

SOURCE 3C A drawing sent to William Cecil in London showing the scene of Darnley's murder. Find the ruins of the house, the bodies of Darnley and his servant, and the four labelled objects

What should Elizabeth do with Mary?

Mary had lost her kingdom, but Elizabeth had her problems too:

Mary may have had something to do with Darnley's murder.	➡ Should Elizabeth put her on trial?
Mary was a Catholic and heir to the English throne.	➡ English Catholics might support her.
She was closely linked to France.	➡ France might help her.
She was Elizabeth's cousin, and a queen.	➡ Elizabeth felt Mary should be treated like a queen.
Protestant nobles now ruled Scotland for the baby James.	➡ They could be useful allies.

Elizabeth could:
- send Mary back to Scotland
- send Mary to France
- keep Mary in prison in England.

3.8 In pairs, work out arguments for and against each of Elizabeth's three choices. Then have a class vote on what Elizabeth should do with Mary. *AT 1.5*

A WIDER WORLD

Threats at home – 'The monstrous huge dragon'

Elizabeth put Mary in prison in England. In 1571 the first serious Catholic plot to murder Elizabeth and put Mary on the English throne was discovered. Things soon became very difficult for all English Catholics.

SOURCE 3D

We declare Elizabeth a heretic, and to be excommunicated. Moreover she is deprived of her pretended right to her kingdom, and we order all her people not to obey her instructions or laws.

A Bull (proclamation) issued by the Pope, 1570

SOURCE 3E

*Every person that shall hear Mass shall pay the sum of £67 and suffer imprisonment for a year. [1581]
Any Catholic priest who remains in this realm for more than 40 days is guilty of high treason, and any person who aids a priest shall suffer death. [1585]*

Two laws passed by the English Parliament

SOURCE 3F

I ride daily in the country, hear confession, and after Mass, preach, being greedily heard. I cannot long escape the heretics, they have so many scouts. I wear ridiculous clothes, and often change my name. I find many neglecting their own security to have only care of my safety.

A letter from Edmund Campion, a Catholic priest, to the priests in Rome who sent him to England in 1580

SOURCE 3G
A hiding place for Catholic priests in Sawston Hall, near Cambridge, a Catholic 'safe house'. Priests hid in cramped spaces behind passages, up chimneys, or under the floor, sometimes with no food for several days, while soldiers searched the house for them. Edmund Campion was caught in a hiding place like this at Lyford Grange in Berkshire, and then executed

Most Catholics just wanted to keep to their religion, but a few went on plotting to put Mary on the throne. Parliament begged for Mary's execution, and called her a 'monstrous huge dragon'. For nearly 20 years, Elizabeth kept Mary in prison, and refused to execute another queen, who was her cousin.

In the end, a double agent employed by the Queen's minister, Sir Francis Walsingham, found (or perhaps forged) evidence that Mary was in touch with a rash young Catholic plotter, Anthony Babington. Elizabeth reluctantly agreed that Mary must die. The Scots Queen was executed at Fotheringay Castle on a cold February morning in 1587.

3.9 Take sources 3D–G. Find evidence to explain:
  a why English Catholics had to choose between being loyal to the Pope, and being loyal to the Queen [AT 3.4]
  b why and when it was very dangerous to attend Catholic services [AT 3.4]
  c the experiences of Catholic priests and those who helped them. Is Source 3F likely to be truthful? [AT 3.5]

3.10 Explain why Elizabeth and her Council thought Catholics were traitors, and why Catholics who were executed believed they were martyrs. [AT 2.8]

3.11 In pairs, work out an argument between two English Catholics. One supports Mary Queen of Scots, the other just wants to stick to his religion. [AT 1.6]

3.12 Make an illustrated Protestant poster demanding the death of Mary Queen of Scots, the 'monstrous huge dragon'. [AT 2]

3.13 Make a strip cartoon of the life and death of Mary Queen of Scots. Make clear why Walsingham might want to forge evidence against Mary and why Elizabeth did not want her execution. [AT 1.3]

ELIZABETH I AND HER WORLD

Threats abroad – Danger from Spain

At the beginning of Elizabeth's reign, Philip II, ruler of Catholic Spain, was friendly. He had been married to Elizabeth's sister Mary ◁26 79▷ – and for a time considered marrying Elizabeth ◁31. A friendly England meant the sea route between his lands in Spain and the Netherlands was safe.

Gradually, however, Protestant Elizabeth and Catholic Philip became bitter enemies, and not just because of religion. But both of them were cautious and disliked spending money – Elizabeth avoided trouble as long as she could.

The New World: Philip II ruled an Empire 80▷. As well as the Netherlands, and lands in the Mediterranean, Spain controlled the 'New World' (which they called New Spain) across the Atlantic and its rich resources. Spanish ships sailed home from the Caribbean with cargoes of gold, silver, silk, pearls, emeralds, valuable dyes, and sugar, still a luxury in Europe. But from 1562, Sir John Hawkins traded there too. Soon Francis Drake and other English sailors joined him, and began to attack Spanish treasure ships.

Rich Elizabethans loved miniature pictures, painted with a fine brush in brilliant colours under a magnifying glass. They wore them like jewels, or kept them in a special velvet-lined drawer. This miniature of Sir Francis Drake was painted by Nicholas Hilliard in 1580 to mark his return from his voyage round the world, when the Queen made him a knight.

SOURCE 3H

John Hawkins recently passed Cape St Vincent with 25 well found ships. Drake must be close to the West Indian islands. The ships from New Spain would certainly be loaded and on their way, so that the Englishman will have them at their mercy. And the most annoying thing is that this Hawkins could not have fitted out so numerous and so well equipped a fleet without the secret aid and consent of the Queen.

Letter from a German banker working in Seville, Spain

3.14 Whose side is the banker on? How can you tell? Explain his attitude. *(AT 3.7, 2.3)*

3.15 How useful is Source 3H in showing the importance of Drake and Hawkins' attacks on Spanish ships, and Elizabeth's attitude? *(AT 3.5)*

So Spain and England were enemies for two reasons: religion, and competition for the riches of the New World. Philip now wanted to conquer England – and bring her back to the Catholic faith. These were long-term causes of war. By 1588, events had sparked off war. We call these events short-term causes.

Sparks which led to war

Francis Drake's voyage round the world, 1577–80: Drake captured Spanish treasure in the Caribbean and off Peru, and reached what is now California. The Spaniards called him *El Draque*, the dragon, who seemed to have a magic mirror to see over the horizon and find their ships. On Drake's return, the Queen knighted him, and received five packhorse loads of Spanish treasure.

Help for Dutch Protestants, 1585: In the Netherlands, Protestants were struggling to break free from Spain. Elizabeth sent English soldiers to help the Dutch to fight the strong Spanish army, commanded by the Duke of Parma. The English expedition was not very successful, but it infuriated Philip.

The execution of Mary Queen of Scots: Philip was already building an Armada (invasion fleet) in 1587 when he was shocked by the death of the Catholic Queen. It helped him too – Mary passed on her claim to the English throne to him. Philip was now ready to attack.

3.16 Make an illustrated diagram to show the long-term and short-term causes of war between England and Spain. *(AT 1.5)*

A WIDER WORLD

The Armada

Philip's plan for the Armada

- Sail up the Channel, and join Parma's army in the Netherlands.
- Guard Parma's soldiers as they cross the Channel in barges.
- Land in England and take London. English Catholics would fight for him, and England would become a Catholic country again.

Problems and delays: By the spring of 1587 Philip's Armada was nearly ready in Cadiz harbour. Suddenly English warships led by Francis Drake sailed in, and attacked the Spanish fleet. Drake said he destroyed 37 ships at Cadiz. A Spanish report sent to Philip said 24. Drake also burnt stacks of wood for storage barrels, and when the Armada sailed a year later, many barrels leaked because they were made of the wrong wood. Drake said cheekily afterwards he had singed the King of Spain's beard. But beards grow again – Philip rebuilt his ships. He had other problems though, and so did Elizabeth:

Philip's problems

- Harbours in the Netherlands: none were deep enough for the big Spanish ships.
- Barges: many needed to transport Parma's army to England. They might sink in rough weather.
- Supplies: shortages because the Armada needed so much.

Elizabeth's problems

- The vast size of the Armada: a terrible threat.
- Weak land defences: untrained and badly equipped soldiers. Parma's army was the best in Europe. If it landed, defeat seemed certain.
- Ignorance about Spanish plans: the Armada might land anywhere.
- Supplies: shortages for the English fleet too.

The war of words: In the summer of 1588, Philip's Armada was ready to sail. The Spanish Government published full details, which were printed and sold all over Europe, including England:

- **Ships:** galleons, other fast fighting ships, supply ships: 130
- **Men:** sailors, soldiers, officers and their servants, gunners, doctors, 180 friars and priests. Total: over 30,000
- **Arms:** cannons and small guns: 1,900. Cannon balls: 123,790. Also powder, bullets, pikes, armour, swords
- **Food and drink:** biscuit, bacon, fish, cheese, rice, beans, wine, vinegar, water.

3.17 This sort of information about a fighting force would be Top Secret today. Why did the Spaniards publish it?

3.18 The English published it too, adding such things as whips, thumbscrews, racks, and pincers. Why did they do that?

SOURCE 3I   *An English picture of the attack on the Spanish Crescent near Plymouth*

The Spanish Crescent: The strong warships sailed on the outer rim and the tips, and when attacked, closed in to protect the heavy ships in the centre. Source 3I is an English picture, but it shows how well the Spanish crescent worked. The English had to break it to beat the Armada.

Spanish ships looked bigger because they had high forecastles. They were designed to close in and fight the enemy at close quarters, so they carried a lot of soldiers. In fact the biggest ship in the battle was English. The English ships were faster and low in the water, with better guns, designed to fire at the enemy from some distance. They did not carry soldiers.

The end of the story: On 29 July, when everyone still thought the Armada would land, the Queen visited her troops at Tilbury, near London, and made a rousing speech:

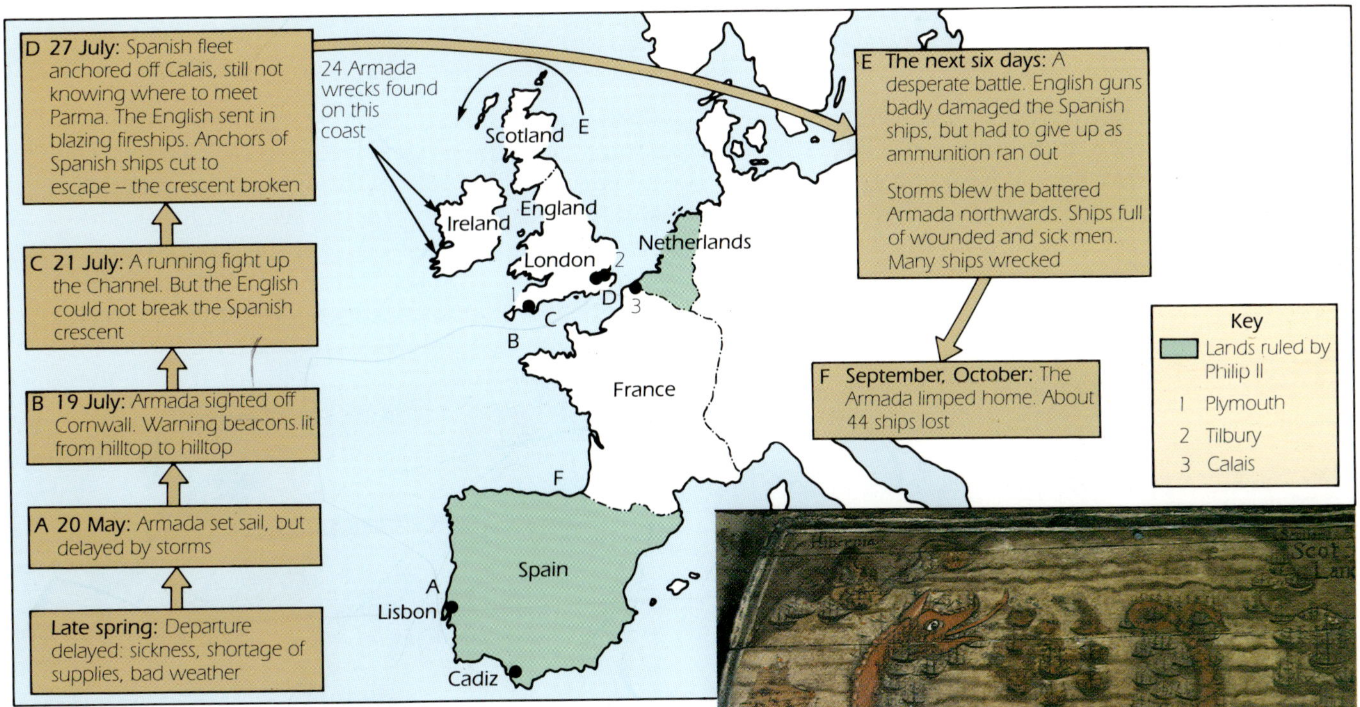
D 27 July: Spanish fleet anchored off Calais, still not knowing where to meet Parma. The English sent in blazing fireships. Anchors of Spanish ships cut to escape – the crescent broken
C 21 July: A running fight up the Channel. But the English could not break the Spanish crescent
B 19 July: Armada sighted off Cornwall. Warning beacons lit from hilltop to hilltop
A 20 May: Armada set sail, but delayed by storms
Late spring: Departure delayed: sickness, shortage of supplies, bad weather
24 Armada wrecks found on this coast
Scotland
E
Ireland
England
London
2
1
D
3
C
B
Netherlands
France
F
Spain
A
Lisbon
Cadiz
E The next six days: A desperate battle. English guns badly damaged the Spanish ships, but had to give up as ammunition ran out
Storms blew the battered Armada northwards. Ships full of wounded and sick men. Many ships wrecked
F September, October: The Armada limped home. About 44 ships lost
Key
Lands ruled by Philip II
1 Plymouth
2 Tilbury
3 Calais

The journey of the Armada, 1588

I am resolved in the midst and heat of battle to live and die amongst you all ... I know I have the body of a weak and feeble woman, but I have the heart and stomach of a king, and a King of England too, and think foul scorn that Parma, or Spain, or any prince of Europe should dare to invade the borders of my realm.

SOURCE 3J **The English view of the Armada: a picture painted about 20 years afterwards. The Armada is an evil crescent-shaped red dragon, bravely attacked by the English fireships. At the top, Spanish ships are wrecked off Scotland (right) and Ireland (left). At the bottom, on the coast of England, victorious English soldiers carry the flag of St George**

Everyone cheered, ready to fight to the death. But we shall never know what would have happened if Parma's army had landed.

The English ships were not so badly damaged, and near home, but were full of sick men too. Many died (probably of typhus) in the streets of English ports, and Elizabeth did not find enough money even to give them their pay. Admiral Lord Howard wrote sadly to the Queen's advisers, 'It would grieve any man's heart to see them that have served so valiantly to die so miserably.'

A great victory?

The English thought the defeat of the Armada was a great victory. Parma's army had never landed, and they were still free, Protestant, and ruled by their English Queen. Nothing changed for English Catholics either, even though they stayed loyal, and did not plot or rebel in 1588. But the war dragged on. Philip rebuilt his Armada and remained a danger to England, especially as he helped the Irish to rebel from 1595.

3.19 Make your own copy of the map. Show Philip's plan in one colour, and the actual route of the Armada in another.

3.20 Decide what part the following played in the defeat of the Armada and arrange in order of importance, with reasons: AT 1.6

- Weakness in Philip's plan
- Shortage of supplies
- No help for Spain from English Catholics
- The weather
- English guns and ships
- No modern communications system
- Elizabeth as a war leader

3.21 What famous legend does Source 3J use, and why? Why has the artist designed his picture like this? How useful is his picture? AT 3.7

3.22 Why did the English and the Spanish disagree over whether the defeat of the Armada was an important English victory? AT 2.5

A WIDER WORLD

Crime, punishment and poverty

Justices of the Peace (JPs, or magistrates) were important people in Tudor England. They were usually local landowners, who had a good deal of control over local people's lives anyway ◁ 11, 14. JPs dealt with everyday crimes, and much of it was stealing, especially late in Elizabeth's reign.

The parish constable had to catch criminals, and carry out the punishments ordered by JPs. It was not an easy job – there were no policemen in Tudor England.

Punishments were harsh. A man convicted of forgery had the letter F branded on his face. The penalty for stealing anything worth more than a shilling was hanging (if you were caught). The worst crime was treason, and the terrible penalty was hanging until the victim was not quite dead, then drawing and quartering: the intestines were pulled out, and the body cut in four pieces. A woman guilty of treason was burnt; a nobleman did slightly better – he was beheaded.

A London night watchman. He walked the streets after dark at regular intervals, calling out the time and what the weather was like. He carried his own lantern, because the streets were dark, unless householders provided lights. You can work out why he needs the other equipment he carries

Fear of witches increased in Tudor times. An unpopular old woman was often accused, especially if she had a 'familiar' – a cat, a mouse, or even a beetle, thought to be a demon who would carry out her orders. One test was 'swimming a witch'. The unfortunate woman in this picture floated, and that proved to the onlookers that she was a witch, so she was executed. The sinister pig on the bank is meant to be her familiar

Sturdy rogues

People in trouble with the law were often poor. The rich did not think much of 'sturdy' poor people, who were healthy, but unemployed, and often wandered from place to place looking for work. So these 'rogues' were often in trouble, blamed for being lazy or drunk, and out to beg and steal.

Standing in the pillory in the street was a common punishment. This picture in a cheap ballad sheet shows a beggar caught daubing his face with oxblood and pretending he had been run over, to make people feel sorry for him. He had bought a house and land in Kent with his takings

> SOURCE 3K
>
> *All strange [not local] beggars now being within the city to the common nuisance shall leave this city within 24 hours upon pain of punishment in scourging [whipping] of their bodies.*
>
> A rule in York in 1530, common in many Tudor towns

ELIZABETH I AND HER WORLD

SOURCE 3L A picture in a Tudor pamphlet showing what people thought wandering beggars were like. Is the man really lame?

SOURCE 3M

Ann Buckle of the age of 40 years, widow, hath two children, one of the age of 9 years and the other of 5 years that work lace, and hath dwelt here ever. No alms, but very poor.

John Burr of the age of 54 years, glazier [puts glass in windows], very sick and work not, and Alice his wife ... 40 years that spin, and have 7 children, who spin wool and have dwelt here ever – in his own house, no alms, indifferent [not quite so poor as the others].

John Findley, of the age of 82 years, cooper [barrel maker] not in work, and Joan his wife, sickly, that spin and knit, and have dwelt here ever – in the church house, very poor.

3.23 How can you tell that the artist in Source 3L doesn't want you to be sorry for this family? *AT 3.3*

3.24 How useful are Sources 3K and 3L in telling you about: *AT 3.6*
   a what the poor were like?
   b what better-off people thought of the poor?

3.25 Make an illustrated flow chart showing what happens to a beggar caught stealing in a Tudor town. *AT 3.4*

Hard times in the 1590s

- War with Spain dragged on
- Prices rose. Wages did not
- Many unemployed. Ex-soldiers and sailors increased the numbers
- A riot in Oxfordshire against enclosures ◁16 and high prices, 1596
- Cold wet summers and very bad harvests, 1594–7
- Famine amongst the poor, 1596–7.

Poor people in Norwich

Richer people also began to realise that some people could not help being poor. In 1570 the prosperous businessmen who ran the city of Norwich were worried by the numbers of poor people in the city. They wanted to help them, but they did not want 'idle rogues' crowding into the city in search of help too.

So they made a census – a list of the poor who lived in Norwich and 'dwelt here ever'. It recorded help the city was already giving them, either that they were receiving alms (money or food), or living in the 'church house'. Source 3M describes three families in the 1570 census.

3.26 Why were the families in Source 3M poor? *AT 3.3*

The Poor Law of 1601

In 1601, Parliament passed a 'Poor Law', which tried to deal with the problem of poverty:

- The old, the sick, and young children were to be given alms, or shelter in the local 'poor house'.
- Healthy people, able to work, were to be given materials to work with – such as wool or flax.
- Money to pay for both kinds of help was collected from a local tax called a 'rate'.
- Those refusing to work were to go to prison.

This law lasted for over 200 years. It worked quite well if local people were generous. It certainly did not cure poverty, but it was a beginning.

3.27 What kinds of poor people are described in this section? How and why did the Poor Law of 1601 aim to help them? *AT 1.3*

3.28 a Discuss the causes of the Poor Law of 1601, and why the ruling classes felt something had to be done about poverty. *AT 1.5*

b Discuss the reasons why people were poor in the 1590s, and are poor in the 1990s. *AT 1.4*

A WIDER WORLD

Elizabethans enjoy themselves

London theatregoers

Going to the theatre was an exciting new entertainment in Elizabeth I's reign. Before that people had watched plays in inn-yards, or the marketplace. The Globe, finished in 1599, was the most famous of the new London theatres.

The Globe was even more exciting because a young actor called William Shakespeare was writing most of the plays performed there. Rich and poor Londoners laughed at his comics, sympathised with the heroes and heroines, and wept at the tragedies. Audiences were much noisier than they are now. Women enjoyed the theatre as well as men, but they did not act – boys played the female parts.

Some people disapproved of the theatre, especially when plague was about:

SOURCE 3N

Behold the sumptuous theatre houses, a continuous monument to London's extravagance and foolishness ... The causes of plagues is sin; the cause of sin are plays: therefore the cause of plagues are plays.

A Puritan preacher in London, 1578

SOURCE 3P

Stage-plays give opportunity to evil and ungodly people to meet and plan to make trouble. They are places for tramps, thieves, horse-stealers and other idle and dangerous persons to meet. They maintain idleness and draw apprentices and other servants from their ordinary work, and all sorts of people from sermons. In times of sickness, other persons are infected.

The Lord Mayor of London's letter to the Queen's Council, 1597

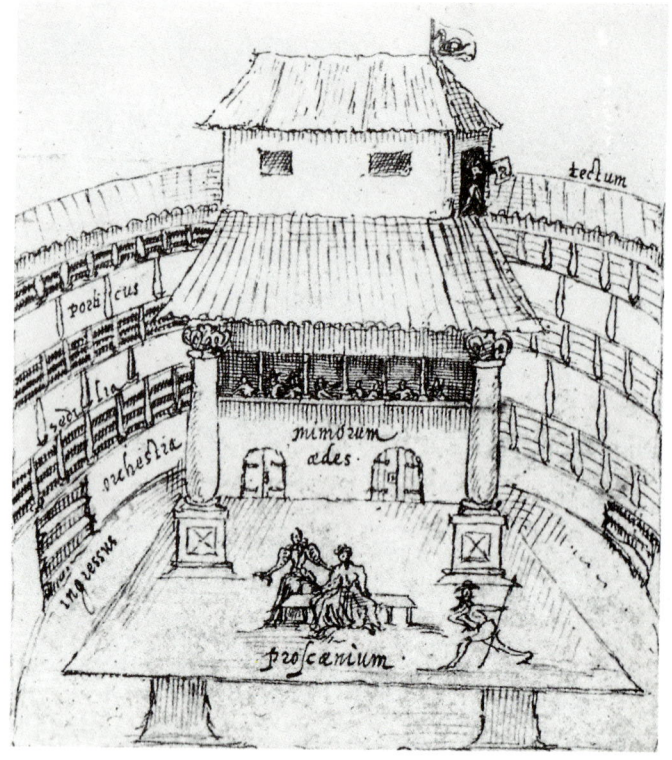

A sketch drawn at the time of the Swan Theatre, which was very like the Globe

3.29 Why do the writers of Sources 3N and 3P want to stop plays? Do they agree with each other? What do they tell you about Elizabethan London?

3.30 Draw your own labelled plan of the Globe Theatre, and write a description of a visit there – perhaps to a play by Shakespeare.

AT 3.4

London in about 1600 – its population had grown from 50,000 in 1500 to 200,000, and it was still expanding

ELIZABETH I AND HER WORLD

Music and other pleasures

Elizabethans were good at entertaining themselves – they had to be, without modern TV or radio. The guests at the feast in Source 3Q are watching a masque – a musical procession in fancy dress. The god Mercury with wings in his hat, and the moon goddess Diana lead the actors wearing red masks. Soon everyone will join in the singing and dancing.

The musicians are a 'broken consort', playing wind and string instruments: (clockwise) a flute; two instruments plucked like a guitar – a lute with gut strings, and a cittern with metal strings; a bass viol (like a cello); a pandora strung with metal; and a violin.

Madrigals were songs with different parts in a complicated beautiful pattern. Elizabethans often sang madrigals with their guests and servants, and were surprised if anyone could not manage it. Listen to some Elizabethan music if you can – it is better than reading about it in a book.

Other indoor entertainments were chess, backgammon (found on the *Mary Rose* ◁6▷), different kinds of card games, and nine men's morris, a board game a bit like noughts and crosses.

Elizabethans could be very rowdy. This is a description of a village festivity at Christmas:

SOURCE 3R

The wildheads of the parish bedeck themselves with scarves, ribbons, and laces, hanged all over with gold rings, and other jewels; they tie about either leg twenty or forty bells, with rich handkerchiefs in their hands. Then march this heathen company towards the church, their pipers piping, their drummers thundering, their stumps dancing, their bells jingling, their handkerchiefs swinging above their heads like madmen, their hobby-horses and other monsters skirmishing amongst the crowd.

Football was a terrifying game without rules, played in the streets, and a good excuse for a rough and tumble fight. There were rules in towns forbidding archery practice in the streets – not always obeyed. Noisy audiences watched bull and bear-baiting when they had the chance.

3.31 What can you learn about table manners, furniture and costume from Source 3Q? [AT 3.3]

3.32 What is going on in Source 3R? Does the writer approve? How can you tell? [AT 3.3]

3.33 Make an illustrated folder or frieze of Elizabethan entertainments.

SOURCE 3Q
Sir Henry Unton, an Elizabethan gentleman, entertains his guests to a feast and a masque in his house in Oxfordshire in the 1590s

4 Crown and Parliament

James I

In the cold spring of 1603, Elizabeth I died and James VI of Scotland became James I of England [79]. So the Scots gave England a Stuart king – but the two kingdoms stayed separate, and did not get on any better [13].

James I's new subjects were excited to have a king again, with two sons. (Elizabeth's strong character had not changed people's attitude to women in power.) But James was very different from Elizabeth. He was undignified, afraid of crowds, and the Scots who came with him were not popular.

SOURCE 4A

He was of middle stature, his doublets quilted to be dagger-proof, his breeches in great pleats, full stuffed. He was naturally timid, his eyes large, rolling after any stranger that came into the room, his beard very thin, his tongue too large for his mouth, his legs very weak ... he was the wisest fool in Christendom ... wise in small things, but a fool in weighty matters.

Anthony Weldon, an English courtier dismissed by James for insulting the Scots

James wrote a book about the divine right of kings – the idea still accepted by most people, that a monarch's power came from God, and must be obeyed. James was tactless about it – in 1610, when Parliament would not vote him enough money, he told them, 'Kings are not only God's lieutenants upon earth, and sit upon God's throne, but even by God himself they are called gods'.

James I was not so interested in grand portraits as Elizabeth I. This small miniature by Elizabeth's artist Nicholas Hilliard was painted soon after he became King of England

He was also lazy, and preferred hunting to working. His court had a bad reputation for drunkenness, and he spent too much money, especially on his favourites.

James had good points too. He was clever, and had made a good job of ruling Scotland. He wanted peace, and stopped the expensive war with Spain that had dragged on since the Armada. He wanted to be fair to both Catholics and Puritans [28]. Unlike most English people, he wanted England and Scotland to be one kingdom.

4.1 How useful is Source 4A? Explain your answer.

4.2 Make a list in two columns of James's good and bad points. Put stars by the ones which might make him unpopular with the English.

INVESTIGATION

Why did trouble between the Stuart kings and Parliament lead to war?

Key Sources
- Portraits, cartoons, playing cards
- Hollar's picture of Westminster
- Government records

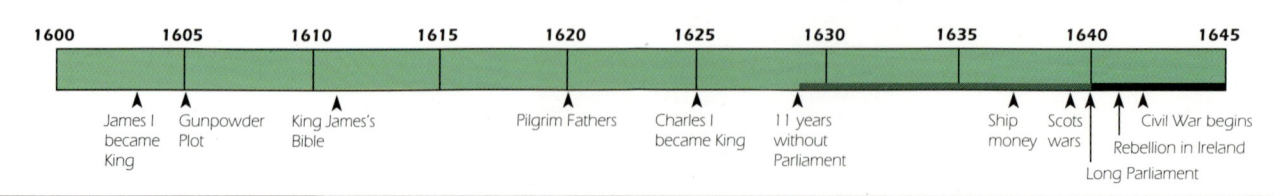

Timeline 1600–1645:
- James I became King
- Gunpowder Plot
- King James's Bible
- Pilgrim Fathers
- Charles I became King
- 11 years without Parliament
- Ship money
- Scots wars
- Rebellion in Ireland
- Long Parliament
- Civil War begins

The Gunpowder Plot, 1605

The plan
To blow up the House of Lords when the King came to open Parliament, and everyone important was there. To kidnap the royal children and take over the government.

Stage 1
The plotters rented a house near Parliament and began to dig a tunnel into a cellar right under the House of Lords. But they came up against a wall almost a metre thick. They gave up, and found they could rent the cellar.

In Westminster's busy streets, no one saw any earth from the tunnel being removed, and it has never been found. The plotters had no difficulty in renting this well-placed cellar.

Stage 2
The plotters put 36 barrels of gunpowder in the cellar, hidden under piles of firewood.

People could only buy gunpowder with a government licence from the Tower of London. Records of licences for this time are missing. And how did the plotters take 36 barrels into the cellar without anyone seeing?

Stage 3
On 26 October, Lord Monteagle received a mysterious unsigned letter. You can puzzle out this important sentence in it, if you remember 's' often looks like 'f', and the spelling is odd.

yet i saye they shall receyue a terrible blowe this parleament and yet they shall nat seie who hurts them

Monteagle went to Cecil, who told the King. The government said this letter was from Thomas Tresham, Lord Monteagle's brother-in-law.

Lord Monteagle seemed to know that this sentence meant that there would be an explosion which would blow everyone sky high during the opening of Parliament. Experts think the letter may be forged.

Stage 4
Guy Fawkes, a Yorkshire soldier, was in the cellar on the night of 4 November, waiting to set light to the gunpowder. Guards searched the cellar and found him. He was taken to the Tower and tortured. After four days he told the whole story.

The government official who owned the cellar died suddenly on the morning of 5 November.

Stage 5
Soldiers arrested the other plotters. Some were shot – the two leaders, Catesby and Percy, with the same bullet. The others were hanged, drawn and quartered in January 1606, including the poor tortured Guy Fawkes. Tresham was put in the Tower, and suddenly died there in December 1605, no one knows how.

Catesby, Percy and Tresham may all have known more than the other plotters.

4.3 In pairs, work out your explanation of the mysteries in the Gunpowder Plot. *AT 1.4 2.4*

4.4 What do you think it was like for Catholics who were not plotters, after the Gunpowder Plot? *AT 1.3*

4.5 Why did 5 November become a day of celebration every year? Should we still celebrate it? *AT 1.6*

The conspirators in the Gunpowder Plot were resentful because James did not help Catholics, as they had hoped. Their story is puzzling. James's minister, Robert Cecil, may have discovered the plot quite soon, and allowed it to go ahead, to frighten the King, and to make sure he kept the laws against Catholics. If that was what Cecil wanted, he succeeded

A WIDER WORLD

Puritans and pilgrims

Puritans wanted
- Plain and simple church services, with sermons (long ones) to teach the Bible.
- Plain church buildings, with no candles, pictures, statues, or stained glass in windows.
- No bishops to order people about – or bishops with much less power.
- No games or sports on Sundays, which was for church-going. Some Puritans disapproved of fashionable dress, men wearing long hair, and amusements like the theatre and horse-racing.

Puritans were English Protestants who wanted to 'purify' the Church of England ◁28 . They thought it was much too like the Catholic Church, and they hated and feared Catholics. They got their nickname in Elizabeth's reign. The Queen refused to listen to them, because she did not want any more changes in the Church of England. James I was more sympathetic, and held a meeting at Hampton Court in 1604, with one important result – a fine new English translation of the Bible, usually called **King James's Bible.** But the Puritans got none of the changes they wanted, and some were so disappointed that they decided to leave England.

The Pilgrim Fathers

The Pilgrim Fathers were a group of Puritans who decided to make the long dangerous journey to North America, to set up a 'New England' with a Puritan Church. In 1620 they set sail from Plymouth, in a small ship called the *Mayflower*, with 103 people crammed on board and all the equipment they needed for their new life. They were not all Puritans. Some went to make their fortunes, and perhaps some of the Puritans hoped to do that too.

Over half the Pilgrims died in their first difficult year. The survivors founded the colony 80▷ of 'New England'. Colonies bring many problems – especially to the people who already live in the area, and do not want to lose their land and culture. Pilgrims and native Americans found it difficult to live together, but people descended from both groups are now part of the modern American nation.

4.6 Does Source 4B give us useful evidence about the Pilgrim Fathers? [AT 3.5]

SOURCE 4B **A picture of the time showing Puritans leaving England**

CROWN AND PARLIAMENT

Charles I

SOURCE 4C   Charles I's court painter was Anthony Van Dyck, one of the best artists in Europe. This painting is bigger than lifesize, and everything in it reminds you that Charles is a powerful king – even the loyal courtier gazing up at him. Notice how cleverly Van Dyck has painted the horse as it moves through the arch towards you

Charles I became King in 1625. He was dignified and reserved, very different from his father 79. He was artistic, and collected many beautiful pictures. He was very religious, and devoted to the Church of England.

He was also very bad at understanding how his subjects were feeling, and did not think it mattered anyway. He believed in the divine right of kings 42, and that his power came from God, so he did not have to ask anybody's advice unless he wished to do so. He was soon in deep trouble with his powerful subjects in Parliament.

His marriage made matters worse. His wife was a lively, elegant French princess, Henrietta Maria, and Charles became devoted to her. She was Catholic, and English feelings against Catholics had certainly not changed. She never really understood her new country, and she urged Charles to be a strong King. She soon became very unpopular.

4.7 How does Source 4C:
  a make us forget that Charles I was only just over five foot tall?
  b show him as a powerful king?

AT 2.5

45

A WIDER WORLD

Eleven years without Parliament

Parliament grows more important

Money: Elizabeth I was short of money, and things got worse under James I and Charles I. They had to ask Parliament more often for extra taxes. So MPs could criticise the way money was spent, and refuse to grant taxes, if they did not like the way the King governed.

Religion: The Tudors had used Parliament to make the great changes in religion. Now MPs always wanted a say over religion. Many of them were strong Puritans.

The House of Commons was more important. MPs chose their Speaker; he decided who should speak and what should be discussed. Tudor Speakers were careful to please the crown, but Speakers became more independent under the Stuarts.

Privilege: MPs had the right to speak freely in Parliament, and could not be arrested for anything they said there. They guarded this privilege fiercely.

BUT the King
- made all important decisions
- chose his ministers
- decided when to summon and dismiss Parliament.

Money troubles

Charles I, like his father, spent too much money, for instance on his great art collection. He also had no intention of sharing his power, and in 1629 he decided to rule without Parliament, at least for a time. But now he had to find ways of raising money without asking Parliament, and none of them were popular. Most trouble came from a new tax.

John Hampden and Ship Money: Charles wanted to build more ships for the navy, and had the right to tax ports to pay for ships. In 1635, he made the whole country pay 'ship money'. Most people thought this was just another way of raising money without Parliament.

John Hampden was a Buckinghamshire landowner. He was a Puritan, and much respected – not the kind of person to break the law. He refused to pay ship money and was put on trial before 12 of the King's judges in London. Seven found him guilty – probably to please the King – but nothing more happened. Most people thought Hampden had won. But for the moment, Charles had just enough money, as long as he did not spend anything extra – on a war for instance.

4.8 Use the box above to list reasons why Charles I and Parliament were on a collision course. *AT 1.5*

4.9 Why was John Hampden's case important? *AT 1.4*

SOURCE 4D A Puritan lawyer, William Prynne, had his ears cut off because he wrote a pamphlet against bishops. This cartoon of Archbishop Laud eating ears for dinner shows what Puritans thought of this cruel punishment

An unpopular archbishop

Charles I's Archbishop of Canterbury was called William Laud. He was hard-working and sincere, but also tactless and fussy. The King and Archbishop both disliked Puritans, and thought they caused trouble. They wanted Church of England services to be more dignified, with beautiful music, candles on the altar, and more statues and pictures in church – all the things Puritans hated because they seemed Catholic.

When Laud and his bishops enforced these changes, Puritans blamed them for changing the Church of England, and were worried that bishops were getting too powerful.

Charles I remained firmly Church of England, but he seemed to favour Catholics at court, and apparently never realised that people were upset by Queen Henrietta Maria's Catholic priests, and the beautiful new Catholic chapel specially built for her services. All sorts of fears and rumours about a Catholic take-over grew during the 1630s – Catholics were still the bogeymen for many people in Charles I's England.

Trouble in Scotland

Charles I was King of Scotland as well as England, but he did not go there for ten years, and the Scots felt neglected. Then, in 1637, he ordered the Scots to use the Church of England Prayer Book. But many Scots agreed with English Puritans ◁32 and did not want to be ordered about over religion.

The Scots felt so strongly they decided to fight. Now Charles had landed himself with a war he could not pay for. He had some soldiers, but they were badly equipped, did not want to fight the Scots, and ran away when a battle looked likely.

By 1640, the Scots occupied Newcastle and insisted Charles had to pay for their army. He could only do one thing – call Parliament, and hope they would agree to give him the money he needed. The 'Long Parliament' (it lasted officially for 20 years) had the upper hand at last when it met in November 1640.

4.10 Why did Laud's ideas upset Puritans? What else about Charles I upset them? Make a Puritan cartoon about the King and the Archbishop. Underneath write the comments Laud might have made about it.

A riot in St Giles Cathedral, Edinburgh on the first Sunday the Prayer Book was supposed to be used. People are throwing their stools and a good deal else at the bishop. There was trouble all over Scotland

The Arch-Prelate of St Andrewes in Scotland reading the new Service-booke in his pontificalibus assaulted by men & Women, with Cricketts stooles Stickes and Stones,

A WIDER WORLD

Steps to war

The Earl of Strafford was Charles's strongest and most unpopular minister. He had ruled Ireland firmly in the 1630s, and Parliament feared he might bring over an Irish army to help the King

Charles now had to do what the Long Parliament wanted. MPs were determined he would never rule again without them. They imprisoned Archbishop Laud, and accused the Earl of Strafford of high treason. When Charles refused to agree to Strafford's execution, there was a riot outside Whitehall Palace. Violent crowds shouted threats at Charles's unpopular Queen, Henrietta Maria. Charles gave in to save his beloved wife, and Strafford was beheaded.

In 1641, Parliament stopped ship money, and the other ways Charles raised money without asking them. They passed a law saying there *must* be a Parliament every three years, whether the King wanted it or not. They began to attack the Church of England, and this made some MPs fear that Parliament was trying to change too much. Charles began to win some support.

4.11 Look at the box on Parliament on page 46. How much power had Charles lost by 1641?

AT 1.3

Ireland rebels

Problems in Ireland ◁11

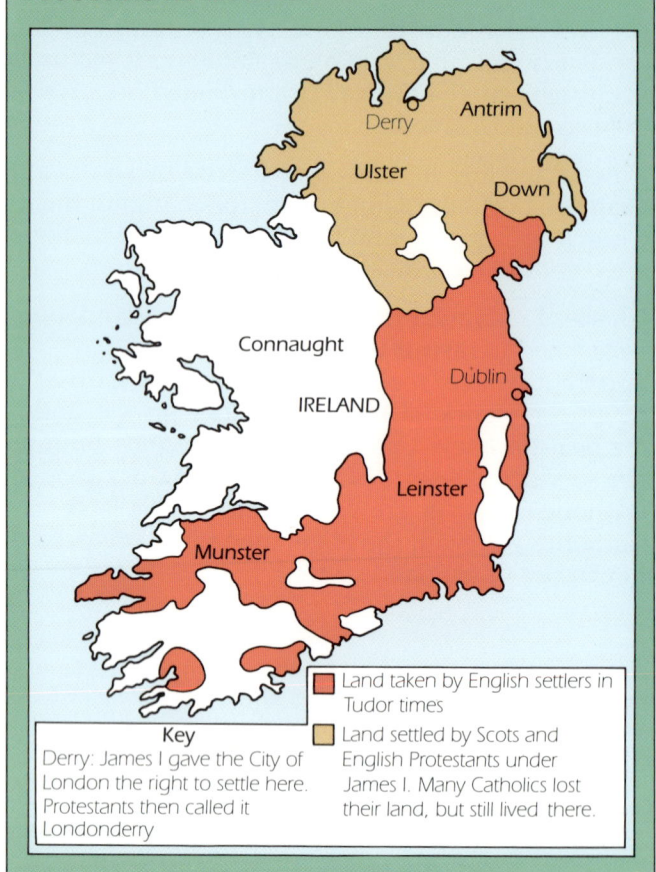

Key
Derry: James I gave the City of London the right to settle here. Protestants then called it Londonderry

■ Land taken by English settlers in Tudor times
■ Land settled by Scots and English Protestants under James I. Many Catholics lost their land, but still lived there.

Religion and land: the two things people minded most about in the Early Modern Age. Ireland remained Catholic after the Protestant Reformation in England ◁28. The Tudors tried to control Ireland by giving Irish land to English Protestant settlers. Irish chieftains led six separate rebellions against Elizabeth I; the worst in the 1590s was not crushed until 1603.

SOURCE 4E

The Irish live like beasts, are more uncivil, more uncleanly, more barbarous in their customs than in any part of the world.

An Englishman reporting in Elizabeth I's reign

The greatest murderers, and the proudest people in all Europe and I am surprised God tolerates them so long in power – I shall say no more, because I shall use all my ink and paper on this subject.

An Irishman on the English

CROWN AND PARLIAMENT

Driuinge Men Women & children by hund: reds vpon Briges & casting them into Riuers, who drowned not were killed with poles & shot with muskets.

SOURCE 4F   There was a terrible massacre of Protestants at a bridge in Portadown in Ulster. This picture is one of a set of playing cards, sold in London soon afterwards. Look at the writing carefully

In October 1641, the Catholic Irish rebelled again. The worst trouble was in Ulster where Catholics took revenge on Protestants who had taken their land.

4.12 Explain the attitudes in Source 4E. — AT 1.6

4.13 Is Source 4F Protestant or Catholic propaganda? How can you tell it is exaggerated? Is it, therefore, useless evidence? — AT 3.8

An army was needed to crush the Irish. But John Pym, the leader of the Long Parliament, feared that Charles might use this army against Parliament. He tried to make a law giving Parliament control of it – he knew that would make Charles powerless.

The Five Members

Henrietta Maria urged Charles to act strongly, and arrest John Pym, John Hampden, and three other important MPs. 'Go pull those rogues out by the ears, or never see my face again!' she is supposed to have said. But it was the privilege of MPs not to be arrested in Parliament [46].

On 4 January 1642, Charles set out with 300 soldiers from Whitehall Palace (**A** in the picture below), five minutes' march to Parliament (**B**). The five leaders had been warned, and quickly escaped by river (**C**) to the City of London, where most people were on their side. The King walked into the House of Commons and said: 'I see the birds have flown'. He asked the Speaker where the five MPs were. The Speaker knelt before the King and replied:

> *May it please Your Majesty, I have neither eyes to see nor tongue to speak in this place but as this House is pleased to direct me, whose servant I am here, and I humbly beg Your Majesty's pardon that I cannot give any answer than this.*

So Charles had to leave, as MPs shouted 'Privilege!' at him. He had tried force, and failed. London was in an uproar, and it was too dangerous for the King and his supporters to stay there. He went north to raise an army. The five members returned in triumph to Parliament. They too began to raise troops. It was clear that if Charles wanted to get back his capital, he would have to fight for it. War soon began.

4.14 Write an eye-witness account by a supporter of John Pym of the attempted arrest of the five members. — AT 2

4.15 Use the headings in this chapter. Decide which are long-term and short-term causes of war between King and Parliament. Draw an illustrated diagram showing long-term causes underneath, short-term causes above, blowing up into war. — AT 1.5

4.16 Do you think that the war was a quarrel about religion? — AT 1.6

Westminster in Charles I's time. The City of London is about half a mile down river

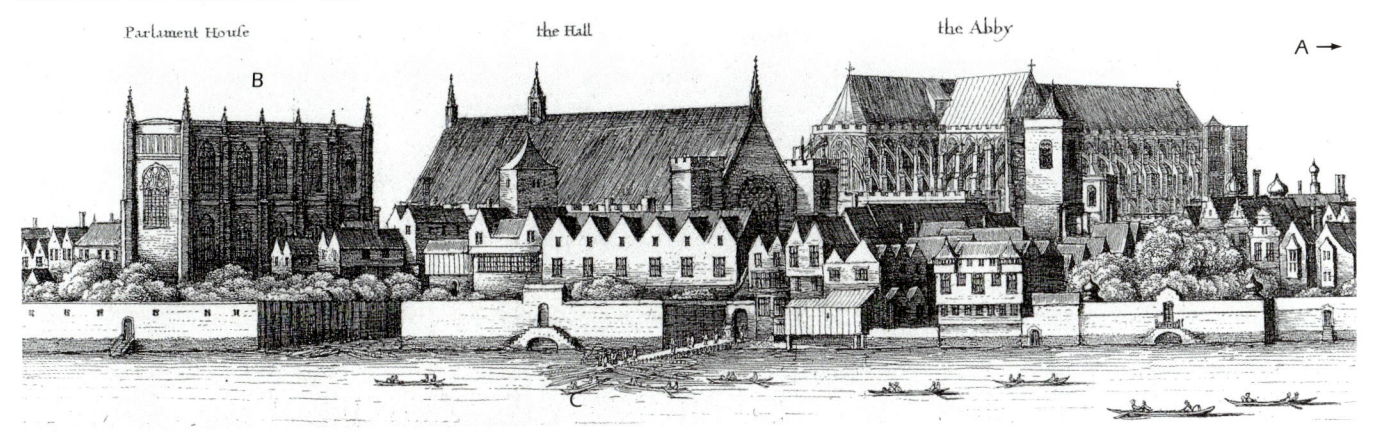

49

5 Cavaliers and Roundheads

The two sides

All wars bring suffering. In the English Civil War, when English people fought each other, families and friends were often split, and people's everyday lives ruined.

SOURCE 5A

This cartoon of 1642 shows the two sides in the Civil War insulting each other with the nicknames that have stuck to them. Cavaliers were the Royalists, loyal to the King. The nickname implied they were like *caballeros*, Spanish for a wild horseman who killed and looted, but Charles I said: 'The valour of Cavaliers hath honoured the name. It means no more than a gentleman serving his King on horseback.'

Roundheads believed they had to defeat the King, to force him to rule with Parliament. Many Roundheads were Puritans – it is said Queen Henrietta Maria first sneered at the 'round heads' of the ordinary Londoners (with short hair) howling for her blood in 1641 ◀48. Rich men usually wore fashionable long hair even if they were Puritans, so not all Roundheads had 'round heads'. They too made the best of it: 'Though we be round-headed, we be not hollow-hearted.'

5.1 Which side is which in Source 5A? How do you know?

A divided family

Sir Edmund Verney was a country gentleman with ten children who lived in Claydon, Buckinghamshire. When war began, he said to a friend who was a firm Cavalier:

SOURCE 5B

You have satisfaction that you are right, but for my part, I do not like the quarrel, and do heartily wish the king would yield. But I have served him near thirty years, and will not do so base a thing as to forsake him, and choose rather to lose my life (which I am sure I shall do).

SOURCE 5C

Brother, what I feared is proved true, which is your being against the King. It grieves my heart to think that my father and I who so dearly love you … should be your enemy … I am so much troubled to think of you being on the side you are that I can write no more, only I shall pray for peace.

Part of a letter written by the third son 'Mun' (Edmund) Verney to the eldest in the family, Ralph, in 1642

INVESTIGATIONS

Who really won the English Civil War?
What was it like to live through war and political change?

Key Sources
- Verney family letters
- Lucy Hutchinson's memoirs
- Oliver Cromwell's letters and speeches
- News sheets
- Records of Charles I's trial and execution

Timeline 1640–1660

- Civil War begins / Battle of Edgehill
- Battle of Marston Moor
- Battle of Naseby
- Second Civil War
- Execution of Charles I
- Campaigns in Ireland and Scotland
- War with Dutch
- Cromwell Lord Protector
- Death of Cromwell
- Charles II returned to rule

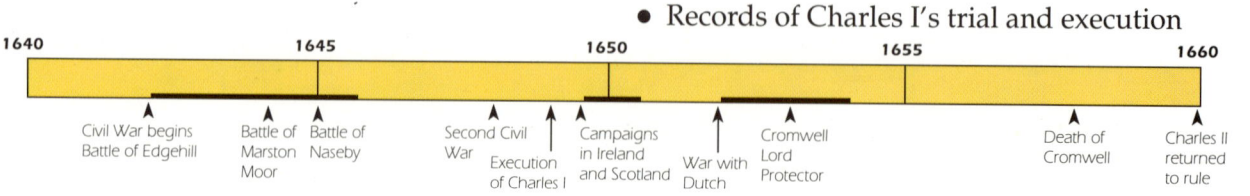

5.2 In Source 5C, which brother is a Roundhead, and which is a Cavalier? `AT 3.3`

5.3 How do Sources 5B and 5C explain why Sir Edmund Verney was so depressed at the beginning of the war? `AT 3.4`

The Verneys had a hard war. Sir Edmund was killed at the battle of Edgehill. He died defending the King's standard (flag) so fiercely that the hand grasping it was cut off. Ralph and his wife had to escape abroad. Mun was killed in Ireland in 1649. Two daughters lost their husbands in the war; five others were stuck at home with no normal chance of getting married.

Many people tried to avoid taking sides altogether, and the lucky ones sometimes managed it, if they lived in a place where there was no fighting. But probably one in ten men chose, or were forced, to join the Cavalier or Roundhead armies, and many women were involved too, as you will see.

England in 1642

Main events

(Important battles shown like THIS.)

The King's aim: to win back London.

1642 EDGEHILL: a draw. The two sides fought to a standstill. The King reached the outskirts of London, but could not capture it, and made his headquarters at Oxford.

1643 Many battles and sieges. The Cavaliers mostly did best, and captured the important port of Bristol, though they failed to get near London.

1644 The Scots joined Parliament. MARSTON MOOR, the first big Roundhead victory, meant the Cavaliers lost the north of England.

1645 NASEBY: a Roundhead victory, and the last great battle of the war.

1646 The King surrendered, and the Roundheads captured Oxford. The war was over.

1648 War broke out again, but the Cavaliers were soon defeated.

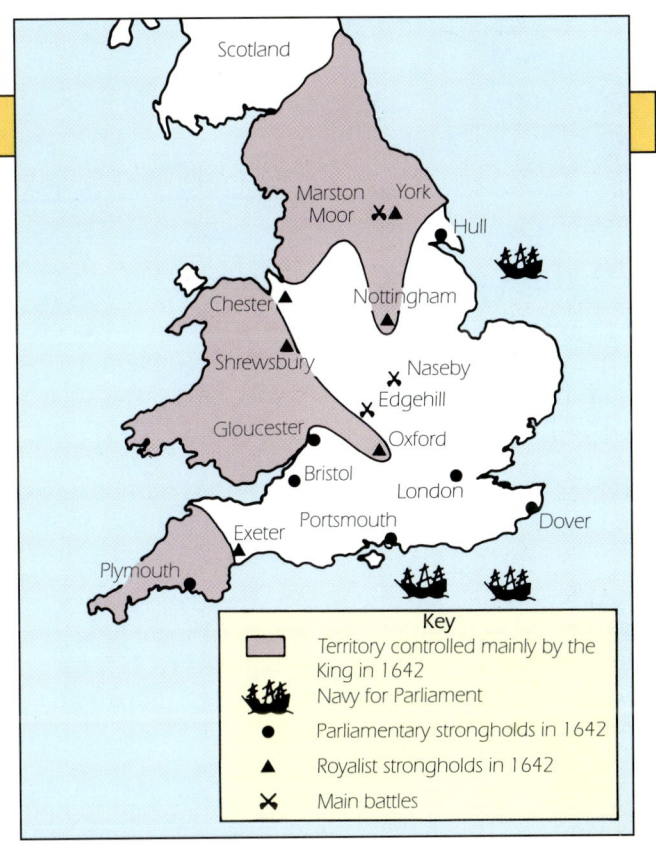

5.4 What advantages and disadvantages did each side have in 1642? `AT 1.4`

	Cavaliers	Roundheads
	in 1642	
People	Mainly Church of England 75 per cent of the nobles Gentry and country people	Mainly Puritan 25 per cent of the nobles Gentry and country people More townspeople
Places	Mainly the north and west Some towns, for example, Oxford, York	Mainly the south and east The capital, London: a big population, trading wealth Ports, for example, Hull, Bristol, Plymouth
Fighting strength	Better cavalry, and more gold and silver to melt down for immediate cash	Not such a strong army The navy helped to bring supplies steadily

A WIDER WORLD

Experiences of war

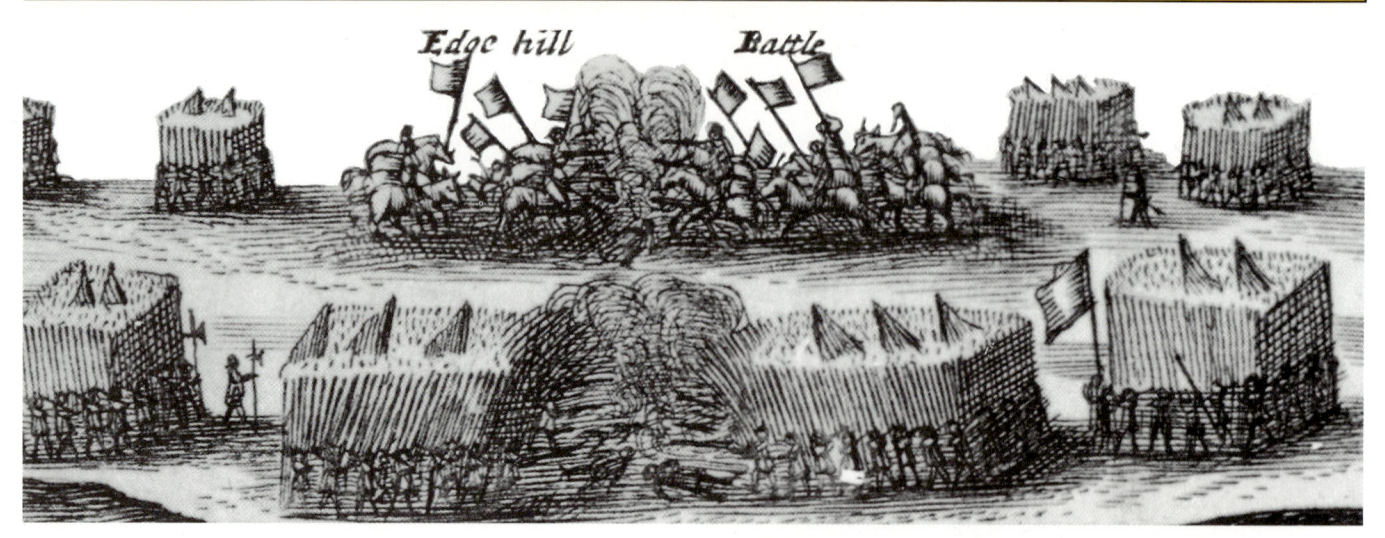

Edge hill Battle

A very tidy picture of the battle of Edgehill from a Royalist pamphlet. Battles were really noisy, terrifying muddles most of the time, and landowners on each side organised their own companies. The standards (flags) helped soldiers to keep together and recognise their own side – few had uniforms. It was considered a disgrace if the enemy captured a standard

Soldiers and weapons

The cavalry (horse soldiers) were the crack troops in an army. At Edgehill, the Cavalier horsemen began the battle with a terrifying charge and nearly broke up the Roundheads – but then galloped out of control off the battlefield, and looted a nearby village. The Roundheads had time to recover, and the rest of the battle was a desperate fight on foot which nobody won.

Musketeers had a difficult job. Their muskets (a gun a bit bigger than a modern rifle) were heavy and clumsy, and sometimes failed to fire. It took about a minute to load them – a long time when a cavalry charge is thundering down on you.

Pikemen had to be tall and strong. Their pikes (spears) were 4–5 metres long, and they had to hold them firmly against a cavalry charge – or advance with pikes lowered like a moving spiky hedge.

Cannons were heavy and difficult to move. They used about 1,300 kilos of shot in a battle, and could cause a lot of damage, but still often missed their target. There were cannons at Edgehill, though not in this picture.

5.5 *Find each kind of soldier in the battle picture.*

The wounded were lucky if they survived. There were no hospitals, and few doctors with the armies. Their usual treatment was bleeding or purging (giving a medicine which caused vomiting and diarrhoea); neither helped a badly wounded man. Surgeons had to amputate badly torn limbs on the battlefield, and you know what operations were like before anaesthetics.

Many women who went to war with their men provided much better care. Lucy Hutchinson's husband was the Roundhead Governor of Nottingham Castle, and she used her own ointments and medicines to help the wounded there, and insisted on caring for Cavalier prisoners too. Her patients recovered.

Soldiers and local people

> **SOURCE 5D**
>
> For hay, grass, and wood £10 ◁3
> William Maynard's bill for bread, beer,
>   hay, grass, wood £5 5s 6d
> Soldiers lodging with villagers £9 9s 6d
>
> A bill sent to Parliament in 1646 by villagers in Charlescombe, near Bath. They had not been paid for the visit of Roundhead troops in 1643

Oxford was a busy crowded city in peacetime. When it became the King's headquarters it was crammed to bursting. A list of houses in one street, St Aldate's, shows that in 1643, in 74 houses, there were 408 *extra* people. An old widow, Elizabeth Treadwell, had three soldiers living in her tiny two-roomed house. We know many ordinary Oxford

CAVALIERS AND ROUNDHEADS

citizens were Roundheads, and the Royalist army brought other problems too:

Disease: There were serious 'plagues' in Oxford in 1643 and 1644 – probably typhus – and both soldiers and townspeople died.

Fire: In 1644 a bad fire destroyed over 200 houses in a poor area of the city. It is said that a careless soldier started it, roasting a pig he had stolen.

Law and order: Drunks caused so much trouble that the King ordered inns to close in the evenings. There was a gibbet in the city centre to hang criminals.

5.6 In Source 5D, make a list of things the soldiers had not paid for. What kind of troops were they? What problems would their visit cause?

5.7 Describe the problems Elizabeth Treadwell must have had in 1643–4.

5.8 Make a list of the things you would dislike if you were a seventeenth-century soldier. Is there anything you would like?

▲ The King at war. Like most soldiers he is protected by a thick leather buff coat or tunic (his is grander than most) and a breast plate. A battle is going on in the distance, and he is dictating a message to his secretary. Notice the writing equipment

Local people hated having armies around, and this cartoon shows one of the reasons. Soldiers were paid less than farm labourers, and often were not paid at all; they also had to find their own food. What has this one been up to?

A WIDER WORLD

Women in wartime

The war changed the lives of many women. Lucy Hutchinson [52] and many others went to war with their men. Some took the chance of adventure and independence, which they had never had before. Elizabeth Alkin, nicknamed 'Parliament Joan', cared for the wounded like Lucy Hutchinson. She washed them, cut their hair, mended their clothes, and made sure they were comfortable by finding hammocks, wood and candles, paying for a good deal herself. She later became a Roundhead spy, hunting out Royalist pamphlets, and wrote pamphlets herself.

Wartime news sheets told stories of 'she-soldiers' – women who disguised themselves as soldiers, like 'Mr Clarke', who joined the Roundhead army with her husband. She fired a musket, wrestled, drank and smoked tobacco like the other soldiers, and even hid her pregnancy until she actually produced a baby son

Some wives stayed at home to keep things going, and if there was fighting in the area, they sometimes had to fight too.

The Royalist Lady Bankes, mother of ten children, defended Corfe Castle in Dorset twice against Roundhead sieges – her husband was in Oxford with the King, and died there. In June 1643, 600 men attacked Corfe. Their commander was not very impressive – he disguised himself in a bearskin, and crept around on all fours to avoid being shot, but the troops were well-equipped with firebombs and scaling ladders. Lady Bankes, her six daughters, women servants and five soldiers defended the upper castle, hurling stones and burning coals at the attackers. At last a rumour that a Royalist army was approaching drove them off, and Corfe was saved.

The second siege was at the end of the war, when many Royalist strongholds had already surrendered. Lady Bankes was finally forced to give in because one of her officers changed sides, and pretended to bring in reinforcements, which were in fact Roundhead soldiers. She was allowed to leave safely with her children, but the castle walls were blown up, and trunkfuls of her belongings taken away.

5.9 Design a news sheet which tells the story of either Elizabeth Alkin or Lady Bankes. These sheets were often written as illustrated poems, or you could design it as a strip cartoon.

Prince Rupert

Prince Rupert was the best soldier the Cavaliers had. Although he was young, he had fought in Germany. He was brave and dashing, and a brilliant cavalry commander. He seemed to know just where the enemy was, and how to catch him (though as at Edgehill, he did not always keep control of his horsemen [52]).

Rupert had a big white hunting dog called Boy, who went everywhere with him. The Roundheads soon felt they could never defeat Rupert, and thought his dog put a spell on them. At last, at Marston Moor in 1644, Rupert was badly defeated for the first time. The Cavalier army was cut to pieces, Boy was killed, and Rupert had to escape from the battlefield. He continued to fight energetically for the King, but final defeat came two years later.

CAVALIERS AND ROUNDHEADS

5.10 In Sources 5E and 5F, what does the artist in each case want you to think about Rupert? Use as much of each picture as you can (for example, why is Boy black?).

5.11 Does Source 5F tell you more about Rupert, or about how Roundheads felt about him? Explain your answer.

5.12 We do not know if Rupert ever saw Source 5F. Describe or act an imaginary scene when his servant brings him this cartoon, which he has just bought from a ballad seller. What does Rupert say?

◀ SOURCE 5E   Prince Rupert was the King's nephew, and a typical handsome, long-haired Cavalier. This portrait was painted at the beginning of the war, when he was 23

SOURCE 5F   A Roundhead cartoon making out that Rupert had to hide in a beanfield after Marston Moor (probably untrue). Roundhead soldiers search his luggage, and find Catholic objects – though in fact Rupert was Protestant. Boy seems to have changed colour too ▼

A WIDER WORLD

Oliver Cromwell and the Ironsides

Oliver Cromwell was a Puritan country gentleman from Huntingdon, an MP in the Long Parliament. He had no fighting experience in 1642. At the battle of Edgehill, he was very worried about the Roundhead army. He thought it was just not good enough to beat the Cavaliers.

Cromwell went home to Huntingdon, and began to train his own cavalry. He was determined to make it good enough to beat Prince Rupert, and win the war. He was so successful that Rupert nicknamed him 'Old Ironsides'. The name stuck to his troops because they were solid as iron in a battle. This is how he did it:

- He picked 'men of spirit', who, like him, believed they were doing God's will. Some local Roundheads thought Cromwell should only have gentlemen as officers. This was his answer:

SOURCE 5G

I had rather a plain russet coated captain that knows what he fights for, and loves what he knows, than what you call a gentleman and is nothing else ... if you choose godly honest men to be captains of horse, honest men will follow them.

- He was a strict commander, and orders had to be obeyed.

SOURCE 5H

No man swears but he pays twelve pence; if he be drunk he is set in the stocks or worse ... the counties where they come leap for joy.

A Roundhead newspaper, 1643

- He cared for his troops. 'I have a lovely company', he said proudly of them. He always did his best to see they were paid too. (A trooper was paid 24d a day, and had to find food and equipment for himself and his horse ◀3.)
- He trained his cavalry to charge at a 'round trot' – fast enough to break through the enemy, but fully in control. The Ironsides never charged off the battlefield like Rupert's troops at Edgehill.
- He always chose the right moment in a battle to attack, and he won every battle he fought.

Cromwell's Ironsides became part of Parliament's New Model Army in 1645. This was the first army organised over the whole country; in 1645 it won the Battle of Naseby, the last great battle of the war.

This portrait of Oliver Cromwell by Samuel Cooper is unfinished, but it vividly shows his strong, heavy features, and even his pimples – he apparently told one artist not to leave them out of his picture, or he would not pay him

5.13 You are a shopkeeper in Cromwell's home town of Huntingdon, and a firm Puritan. Write a letter to your wife in 1643 saying why you are pleased that you have joined the Ironsides, as an officer. Show what you think of Cromwell as a commander, using the information on this page carefully.

AT 3.4
AT 1.6

Parliament's victory

Here are some reasons why Parliament won the war:

- The fighting power of Cromwell's Ironsides, and the New Model Army
- Control of London. Its power as the capital and its rich trade made it easier for Parliament to organise the war and pay for it
- The navy. It attacked Royalist supply ships, and safeguarded Parliament's
- Help from Scotland. Their army was well-trained and well-equipped.

The King might have won the war at the beginning, if he had captured London quickly. But it dragged on, he ran out of supplies, and could not keep his armies going. That brought defeat.

5.14 Check your answer to 5.4, and the information on page 51. Make an illustrated time chart of the war, showing events and people, and why Parliament won.

AT 1.5

CAVALIERS AND ROUNDHEADS

Trial and execution

Charles I became a prisoner of the New Model Army, who tried to make a deal with him. But he still believed that God meant him to be a powerful King. So he secretly made an alliance with the Scots (and their army), who thought this was a good way to win control in England. A second civil war broke out in 1648. Cromwell and the Army soon made it a complete disaster for the Cavaliers.

Cromwell and the Army leaders now decided 'Charles Stuart, that man of blood' must die. They could have quietly murdered him, but they decided there must be a public trial and execution. A king had never been put on trial before, and no one knew quite how to do it. A special court was set up. One hundred and thirty-five judges were appointed, but not all turned up. The trial lasted eight days in January 1649.

SOURCE 5I

The said Charles Stuart is a **Tyrant, Traitor**, and a public and implacable enemy to the **Commonwealth** of England.

Part of the charge against Charles I, read at his trial

SOURCE 5J

I have a trust committed to me by God. I will not betray it to answer a new unlawful authority ...
I am not an ordinary prisoner ...
I am not allowed to speak – expect what justice other people will have.

Charles I at his trial

5.15 In Source 5I, check the meaning of key words like **this**. Why did the Army leaders decide to hold a public trial, and use these words? *AT 1.6*

5.16 What was Charles I's attitude to his trial (Source 5J)? *AT 3.3 1.6*

5.17 How many signatures are on the death warrant? How many should there be? Why are some missing? *AT 3.3 1.3*

▲ The chief judge in the court which tried Charles I was a lawyer called John Bradshaw. He wore this bullet-proof hat all through the trial. The King refused to take his hat off for a different reason – to show he had no respect for the court

SOURCE 5K

The death warrant ordering the public execution of Charles I, signed by the judges present at the trial. Bradshaw's and Cromwell's signatures are in the first column ▼

A WIDER WORLD

30 January 1649

On this bitterly cold January morning, the King woke early. He was completely calm, and said: 'I fear not death. Death is not terrible to me.' He put on two shirts, so that he would not shiver with cold, and seem to be afraid.

The scaffold was outside his beautiful Banqueting House in Whitehall Palace, heavily guarded by soldiers, and surrounded by a huge silent crowd. Two disguised executioners waited for the King. Nobody knows who they were, even now. Charles made a short speech – only the people on the scaffold could hear it, but three of them wrote it down. Before he put his head on the block, he said one last word: 'Remember'. The axe fell.

> **SOURCE 5L**
>
> *An unjust sentence which I allowed is punished now by an unjust sentence on me …*
> *All the world knows I never did begin a war first with the two Houses of Parliament. The people's liberty and freedom consists in having government, it is not for having a share in government. A subject and a sovereign are clear different things, therefore I tell you that I am a martyr of the people.*
>
> Part of Charles I's speech on the scaffold

> **SOURCE 5M**
>
> *The Blow I saw given with a sad heart, and at that instant there was such a groan by the thousands then present, as I never heard before, and desire I may never hear again. There was one troop immediately marching to Westminster, and another from Westminster, to confuse the people and scatter them, so that I had much ado to escape home without hurt.*
>
> A 17-year-old boy's eye-witness account

5.18 Find evidence in this section which tells you:
   a that some judges at Charles I's trial were frightened or even disapproving
   b that the Army expected trouble
   c that many people found the execution a terrible experience
   d that Charles still believed he was right – except for one thing (Source 5L and page 48).

AT 3.4 1.6

5.19 Hold a class debate on the motion: 'This class agrees that the Royalists were right to call Charles I a martyr.' Some of you could take the viewpoints of Henrietta Maria, John Hampden, Sir Edmund Verney, Oliver Cromwell, and some could argue from a modern viewpoint.

AT 2.8

The moment after the execution of Charles I – a picture printed soon after by a German artist. (Find some German writing.) He was not an eyewitness, and some of the details are wrong, but he knew about the crowds. Look carefully at them, and find different reactions to the King's death

The world turned upside down

When the King was in prison, there were many new ideas about how the country should be ruled, especially in the victorious Army. **The Levellers** were a group with some very modern ideas for the time. They wanted law courts to be speedy, cheap and fair, and thought Parliament should be elected every year to stop MPs being too powerful. One of them said:

> The poorest he that is in England hath a life to lead as the greatest he: every man that is to live under a government ought by his own consent to put himself under that government.

He meant that even poor men should have a vote, as they do now in modern democracies though Levellers still left women and servants out. But Cromwell thought these ideas were too dangerous, and would split his beloved Army. In May 1649, in a night attack, he caught over 300 Levellers planning a rebellion at Burford in Oxfordshire. They were shut up in the church for three days. Then three were shot, while the rest were forced to watch from the church roof. The Levellers gave no more trouble after that.

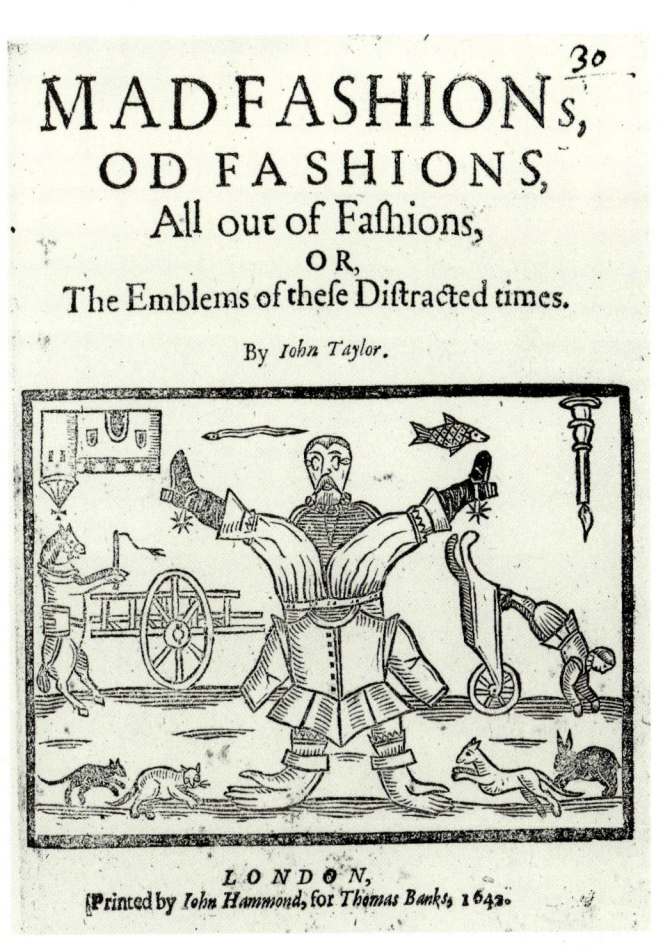

This is the first page of a pamphlet printed at the time of the King's execution, when many people felt the world was being turned upside down. A man walks on his hands, a mouse chases a cat, a rabbit chases a dog ... what else?

The Quakers were founded by George Fox, a weaver, in the 1650s. They treated people as equals, and believed anyone inspired by the spirit of God should speak at their meetings. They had a hard time and were often persecuted. This cartoon is making fun of a Quaker meeting listening to a woman preacher

5.20 Design your own poster dated 1649, with the slogan 'The World Turned Upside Down'.

5.21 What do the events at Burford tell us about Cromwell?

5.22 Why did the ruling classes dislike Leveller and Quaker ideas?

A WIDER WORLD

Sword rule

Now England was without a King – it was a 'Commonwealth' [80] ruled by Parliament. But Oliver Cromwell and his Army had the real power – sword rule. First Cromwell had to be sure the Royalists did not control England's two 'back doors' – Ireland and Scotland.

Ireland

Cromwell was not usually cruel, but he set out to crush Catholic Ireland, and his campaign has never been forgotten there. It was normal then to allow no mercy after sieges, though Cromwell sometimes did. But after the bitterly fought siege of Drogheda in 1649 he reported to Parliament:

> *When they submitted, their officers were knocked on the head, and every tenth man of the soldiers killed; and the rest shipped to Barbados [in the West Indies] … I am persuaded this is the righteous judgment of God upon these barbarous wretches, who have spilt so much innocent blood, and that it will prevent loss of blood for the future.*

Cromwell made sure that his Army stayed in control of Ireland. He took land from 8,000 Irish Catholic landowners and gave it to his soldiers and supporters.

5.23 Why did Cromwell behave like this in Ireland? Do you think it is out of character? [AT 1.6]

Scotland

The Scots hoped to win control in England by supporting the new young King in exile, Charles II. In 1650 Cromwell marched north to deal with them, and won the battle of Dunbar. The next year, 1651, Charles II invaded England with a Scots army. Cromwell caught them at Worcester, where he won his last great victory, which he called his 'crowning mercy'. Charles II escaped to France, and Scotland was a defeated country, occupied by an English army.

Charles II was on the run for six weeks after the Battle of Worcester. Here the King is disguised as a servant, riding at night on a miller's carthorse through an area full of Roundhead troops. Charles was never caught in spite of a reward of £1,000 for 'a tall young man two yards high, with hair deep brown to black'. After he won back his crown in 1660 pictures like this became very popular

King Oliver?

In 1653, Oliver Cromwell became **Lord Protector,** official ruler of England. Like Charles I, he found it difficult to rule with Parliament. For a time Army officers ran local affairs instead of landowners who usually did this. They collected heavy taxes. Some behaved like real Puritans and closed pubs, and stopped horse-racing, and sports on Sundays. Parliament had already abolished Christmas, and closed theatres. People never forgot what it was like to be ruled by soldiers.

In the end, Parliament asked Cromwell to be king, perhaps so everyone would know where they were. We do not know whether Cromwell really wanted the crown, but in the end he refused. He knew most of the soldiers in his beloved Army would never forgive him if he accepted.

The country remained peaceful. Cromwell did not persecute people for their religion (except the Irish) and allowed Jews to live and work openly in England, for the first time since 1290. Countries in Europe respected him, and gave no help to Charles II.

But by 1658, Cromwell was a sad old man. His favourite daughter died. Then he fell ill. On 3 September, the date of his victories at Dunbar and Worcester, Cromwell died.

After Cromwell's death, the world seemed even more upside down. In the end there seemed only one solution – to have a King again. In May 1660, Charles II was invited back to rule his kingdom. Did the Cavaliers win after all? The next chapter will help you to decide.

Oliver Cromwell – Dictator, or Puritan leader?

SOURCE 5N A Royalist view of Cromwell. He stands on a slippery sphere (he will soon fall off), balanced on the mouth of Hell. God's punishment streaks down on to his head. The tree is Britain, and he is ordering it to be cut down. The crown, the Bible, Magna Carta and Parliament's laws crash down with it. The pigs are ordinary people he is leading astray

5.24 Did Cromwell just want power for himself? People who knew him, and historians later, have argued about this. Try to work out your opinion.

- **a** Write a paragraph about each of these headings:
  - Cromwell the soldier
  - The execution of the King
  - Cromwell in Ireland and Scotland
  - Cromwell as Lord Protector
- **b** Discuss the problem in class, and take a vote.

6 Rulers and revolution

A king again

> The way strewed with flowers, the bells ringing, the streets hung with tapestry, the fountains running wine. I stood in the Strand and blessed God. All this was done without one drop of blood shed, and by that very army which had rebelled against him.
>
> John Evelyn's diary, 29 May 1660, when Charles II entered London

The new King was a clever, witty man, very different from his father [79]. Eleven hard years of exile had taught him to hide his feelings, and trust no one. Now he wanted to enjoy himself, and his pleasures included gambling, horse-racing, the theatre and his many mistresses – he probably had 17 children by them.

Charles admired the powerful King of France (see opposite), and probably wanted to rule without Parliament. He also wanted toleration in religion, so people could attend the services they wanted. (He may have been a Catholic himself.) But he knew both those things would upset the powerful ruling classes in Parliament, and he did not want to 'go on his travels again'. To keep his crown he had to:

- rule with Parliament – the laws passed in 1641 stayed [48]. He was short of money too, so he had to keep in with MPs
- support the Church of England. Most people were tired of the Puritans, and still hated Catholics, so the Church of England seemed safe. Clergy, teachers, and holders of jobs in local government all had to swear loyalty to it. Parliament passed harsh laws to punish Puritan preachers, and the old laws against Catholics remained.

Another day of wild enthusiasm – Charles II rides to Westminster Abbey to be crowned. 'I never looked to see such a day as this,' wrote Samuel Pepys in his diary

6.1 Why were people so pleased to have Charles II back? [AT 1.4]

INVESTIGATIONS

Were English monarchs as powerful after 1660? Was there an 'English Revolution'?

Key Sources
- Diaries by Samuel Pepys and John Evelyn
- Mortality bills in London parishes
- Acts of Parliament

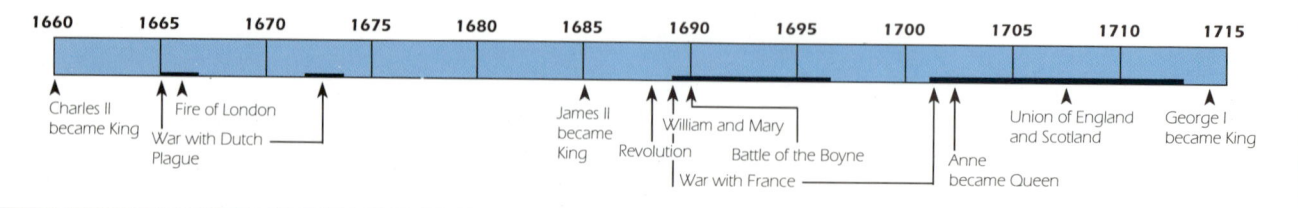

Timeline 1660–1715:
- 1660 Charles II became King
- 1665 War with Dutch; Plague
- Fire of London
- 1685 James II became King
- William and Mary; Revolution
- Battle of the Boyne
- War with France
- Anne became Queen
- Union of England and Scotland
- 1715 George I became King

62

Nonconformists

Puritans had a new name after 1660: Nonconformists – people who did not *conform* or agree with the Church of England. They quietly held to their beliefs, and had most support amongst ordinary people, especially in towns.

John Bunyan (1628–88) was a tinker from Bedford. He and his wife were very poor, but she owned two religious books which had a great influence on him. He became a preacher, and in Charles II's reign he was twice imprisoned for preaching. In prison he wrote the story, *Pilgrim's Progress.* The hero, Christian, goes on a long and dangerous journey from the City of Destruction to the Celestial City.

Two other famous Nonconformists:

William Penn (1644–1718), a Quaker, founded the colony of Pennsylvania in North America.

John Wesley (1703–91) founded the Methodist Church, and wrote many hymns still sung today.

The first page of 'Pilgrim's Progress', published in 1678. John Bunyan is dreaming about Christian setting out on his journey

Changing Europe

The rising power of France: Louis XIV was the leading Catholic ruler in Europe, and wanted to push France's frontiers east into Germany, and north to the Netherlands, and to make his grandson King of Spain. This led to a series of wars which in the end involved England.

The Dutch Republic 80▷**, a new trading nation:** The Protestant Dutch had broken free from Spain (1609) ◁35. Sturdy trading ships, built from materials the Dutch manufactured themselves, made the capital, Amsterdam, an important trading port, and a rival to London. By the 1660s, the Dutch had more trade in the Far East than any other European power, including England.

There were three wars with England over trade between 1652 and 1674. Then a marriage patched things up. **William of Orange,** the ruler of the Dutch Republic, was determined to stop Louis XIV. So he wanted English friendship, and married Mary, the daughter of Charles II's brother James 66, 79▷.

6.2 In Source 6A, how does the artist show Louis XIV as a powerful king? *AT 3.3*

6.3 The English saw Catholic France as their enemy in Charles II's time, rather than Catholic Spain ◁35. Why? *AT 1.4*

6.4 Which sort of English people might be hostile to the Dutch? Why might others be friendly? *AT 1.6*

SOURCE 6A Louis XIV of France – the Sun King – an absolute monarch. This meant he had complete power, and did not rule with a parliament. He built Versailles, the most splendid palace in Europe

A WIDER WORLD

Plague and fire

Things began to go wrong soon after 1660. The Dutch sailed cheekily up the River Medway in 1664, and captured the flagship of the English fleet. Also, two terrible disasters hit London.

Half a million people lived in Charles II's London, many in dark filthy streets, in houses still built of wood and plaster and infested with rats and fleas. The poorest parts were the slums outside the old city walls and along the roads leading into London. Since 1500, there had been several epidemics of bubonic plague, spread by fleas living on the black rat. In 1665 there was a terrible outbreak of plague, and about 150,000 people died. The Londoner Samuel Pepys described it in his diary:

SOURCE 6B

7 June: The hottest day that ever I felt in my life. I did in Drury Lane see two or three houses marked with a red cross upon the doors, and 'Lord have mercy upon us' writ there – which was a sad sight ... I was forced to buy some roll-tobacco to smell and chew.

12 July: A solemn fast day for the plague growing upon us.

12 August: The people die so, that now it seems they carry the dead to be buried by daylight, the nights not sufficing to do it in.

20 September: No boats upon the river; grass grows tall up and down Whitehall ...

16 October: But Lord how empty the streets are ... so many poor sick people in the streets, full of sores ... in Westminster there is never a physician [80]▷, and but one apothecary [80]▷ left, all being dead.

22 November: I heard this day the plague is come very low; that is 600 ... and hopes of a further decrease because of exceeding hard frost.

SOURCE 6C
A picture drawn at the time of the London plague. The huge number of corpses had to be buried together without coffins. The burial pits were supposed to be 1.5 metres deep to prevent dogs digging up the bodies

SOURCE 6D

Deaths from plague in London in 1665, taken from parish lists made at the time:

May:	43	September:	26,230
June:	590	October:	14,375
July:	6,137	November:	3,449
August:	17,036	December:	590

6.5 From Source 6D, make a block graph of London plague deaths in each month.

6.6 How far does Source 6B agree with the evidence from Sources 6C and 6D? Are there differences to explain? *AT 2.6*

6.7 In 1665 people still did not know how plague spread. (Check that you do.) What does Source 6B tell us about how people tried to avoid plague? Take each action, and say how effective it might be. *AT 3.3*

6.8 How useful is the information about the weather in Source 6B? *AT 3.5*

London's burning

Very early on 2 September 1666, a baker's oven caught fire in Pudding Lane in the City of London, and the flames began to spread. Not far away, Samuel Pepys's maid woke him with the news of the fire, but city fires were nothing unusual, and he went back to sleep. The weather was very dry, and a strong wind fanned the flames. When he got up, Pepys soon realised this fire was very serious. By the evening:

SOURCE 6E

With one's face in the wind, you were almost burned with a shower of fire drops. We stayed till it was darkish, we saw the fire as one terrible arch, above a mile long. It made me weep to see it. The churches, houses and all on fire and flaming at once, and a horrid cracking noise the flames made, and the cracking of houses at their ruin.

Samuel Pepys's diary, September 1666

RULERS AND REVOLUTION

Compare this picture of London burning in 1666 with the picture of Tudor London on page 40. Notice which famous London building escaped the fire

The Great Fire of London burned for four terrible days. St Paul's Cathedral and 88 other churches were in ruins. About 13,000 houses were burnt, and 100,000 people were homeless (though Pepys's house was saved). Luckily only a few people died, but a Frenchman, Robert Hubert, was hanged a month later for starting the fire, though it turned out (too late for him) that he was not even in England on 2–5 September.

6.9 In Source 6E, how does Pepys make you feel you are there, watching the fire too? Write your own description of the Fire (bring in smells as well as noise and colour). [AT 3.5]

6.10 Pepys, and many other people, knew how the fire started in Pudding Lane. Why was Robert Hubert blamed? [AT 1.3]

Why did plague die out?

The plague never came back to London after 1665, and soon died out in Europe too. Experts are not sure why. Think about these facts:

- The bacteria which caused plague, and the reasons why they spread, were not discovered until 200 years later.
- The burnt areas of London were rebuilt after the Fire. The new stone and brick houses were cleaner and better built.
- The black rat which carried plague fleas disappeared from Europe about this time – no one knows why. Brown rats flourished but did not carry plague.

6.11 Look carefully at Source 6F. Where did most cases of plague occur, and why? [AT 3.3]

6.12 Is Source 6F evidence that the rebuilding of London was the most important reason why plague died out? Discuss in class, and write down your conclusions. [AT 1.5 3.5]

SOURCE 6F London during the plague and fire

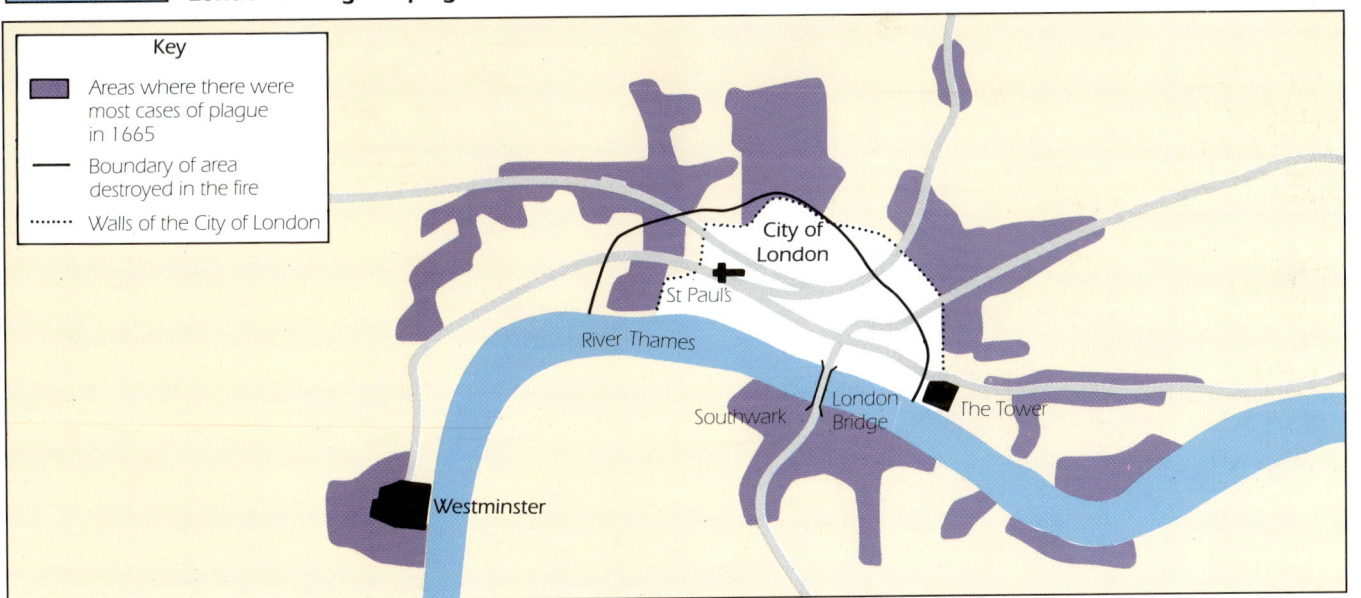

A WIDER WORLD

James, Charles II's brother, with his first wife, Anne Hyde. James was Catholic, but the realistic Charles II insisted that James's two daughters, Mary and Anne, were brought up as Protestants. (Otherwise they learnt drawing, dancing and a little French.) James had courage, but was more stupid than Charles – who defended his brother's right to be the next King, but thought he would be 'obliged to travel again'

This portrait is by the fashionable artist at Charles II's court, Peter Lely. Men now wore wigs – very useful for those going bald or grey. The fashion lasted for over a century

6.13 Make sketches to show differences between Tudor and late Stuart fashions ◁24, 30▷. *AT 1.3*

6.14 Use the Stuart family tree on page 79. What relation was James to: Charles I; Charles II; the two Marys; William of Orange? *AT 1.2*

1688 – It looks like revolution

The problem
Charles II had no legal children. James was his heir ▷79, and was a Catholic. (But his two daughters Mary and Anne were Protestant.)

The first political parties
Whigs (nickname for a sour Scots Presbyterian ◁32) Aim: to stop James being the next king. Against divine right of kings. Wanted to choose another ruler, but could not agree who it should be.

Tories (nickname for an Irish robber) Aim: to keep James as legal heir, because they believed in the divine right of kings. Also strongly Church of England – hoped that as Catholic James was quite old, Protestant Mary would soon be Queen.

Whigs organised this big London demonstration, which burnt a model of the Pope, in 1678. Some Whigs whipped up a great panic that there was a 'Popish Plot' to kill Charles II and put James on the throne

Whig defeat – for a time
Charles II defeated the Whigs. When he died in 1685, James became King peacefully.

King James II, 1685–8
- Catholics were allowed to worship freely.
- Parliament was ignored – especially the laws it had made against Catholics.
- An army with many Catholic officers was kept on the outskirts of London.

A Catholic heir
In 1688 a son was born to James ▷79. The baby would be the next King instead of Protestant Mary, and would be brought up a Catholic.

This playing card is Tory propaganda ▷80. The Tories were desperate to keep Mary as James's heir, and spread rumours that James's son had been born dead, and another baby smuggled into the Queen's room. How does this card encourage that story?

The Queen is brought to bed of a Boy
Reported so

RULERS AND REVOLUTION

Leading Whigs and Tories secretly invited William of Orange, Mary's husband, to bring an army to England against James.

William of Orange

- Ruler of the Dutch Republic
- Strongly Protestant
- Great enemy of Louis XIV of France ◁63.

William was helped by:

- Mary's loyal support – she might have helped her father
- Louis XIV's invasion of Germany in September 1688 – he could not attack William's army as well
- the weather – in November 1688, a 'Protestant wind' blew William's fleet down the Channel to a safe landing in Devon.

---

5 November: The Prince (William) having landed in Torbay ... this put the King and Court into great consternation.

14 November: The Prince increases every day in force. Several Lords go to him. The City of London in disorder.

2 December: The great favourites at court, the Catholic priests, fly ... it looks like a revolution.

18 December: I saw the King take barge to Gravesend – a sad sight! The Prince comes to St James's, and fills Whitehall with Dutch guards. All the world go to see the Prince – he is stately, serious and reserved.

24 December: The King passes into France, whither the Queen and the child were gone a few days earlier.

The diary of John Evelyn, 1688

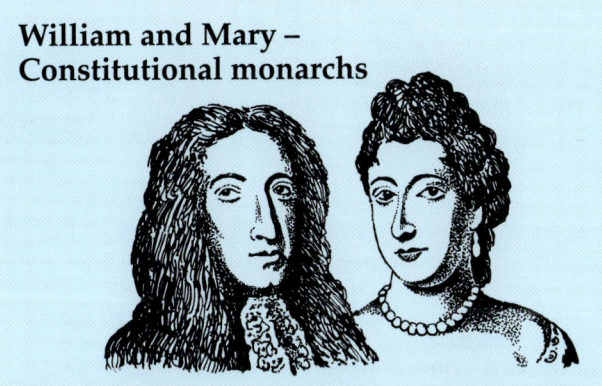

William and Mary – Constitutional monarchs

They agreed to rule as joint equal sovereigns. They were constitutional monarchs, sharing their power with Parliament, because they promised to rule according to laws made by Parliament. The most famous law was the Bill of Rights, 1689.

Religion: The monarch should not be a Catholic, nor marry a Catholic. In 1701 a stricter rule was made: the monarch *had* to be Church of England.

Little change for ordinary people: Catholics had no rights for another century. William agreed with Nonconformists and they were allowed to worship freely. But Parliament ensured that only members of the Church of England could vote, be MPs, attend university and hold the best jobs.

The laws of the land: The monarch had no right to set aside laws made by Parliament, as James II had done.

Parliament: Elections for Parliament had to be held every three years. In 1716, this was changed to seven years.

Money: Britain soon became involved in long expensive wars with France, so the money problem had to be solved. The army and navy were paid for out of taxes agreed by Parliament. Money voted for other royal expenses was called the Civil List. (Parliament still votes for a Civil List today.)

The army: The monarch commanded the army, but Parliament voted the money to run it, so they had some control. William and Mary could still make important decisions, and choose their ministers.

Royal power checked

Wars with France continued on and off for the next century. They were expensive, and Parliament kept control of the money needed. So Parliament also controlled how it was spent, and took a greater part in making important decisions.

Shortage of royal children: William and Mary had no children. Anne (ruled 1702–14) had 17, who all died. Parliament did not want James II or his son back, and chose a distant cousin as the next heir: **George**, Protestant ruler of Hanover, a small state in Germany 79▷. The present royal family is descended from Hanoverian George.

67

A WIDER WORLD

The United Kingdom of Britain

George I (1714–22) and his son George II (1722–60) were not exciting kings. They were constitutional monarchs and kept the rules laid down after 1688. The country stayed prosperous, and that was enough for most English people in 'Georgian' England.

The two Georges also preferred to spend most of their time in Hanover, where they had absolute power ◁63◁. So the powerful ruling classes in the English Parliament took a greater part in running the country.

6.15 Give a reason in each case why the following led to James II losing his crown: his character; the birth of his son; his religion; his attitude to Parliament; his army.
Now decide which reasons are the most important, and arrange them in order if possible – you may think some are equally important. *AT 1.6*

6.16 Look up the word 'revolution' in the dictionary. Discuss in class why 1688 is sometimes called the 'Glorious Revolution', and whether you agree with this label. *AT 2.5*

6.17 Copy and complete the chart below. What has changed, and what has not changed, between 1500 and 1750? How far is it change for the better? What are the most important differences between 1750 and the 1990s? *AT 1.6*

Sir Robert Walpole was a rich Norfolk landowner and Whig MP, and a tough and successful minister to George I and George II. He built up support in Parliament, managed money carefully, and kept his position for so long (1721–42) that he is sometimes called the first Prime Minister. He worked with a group of ministers called a cabinet

◁11, 46, 48, 49	**Crown and Parliament**		
	1500 **Monarchy**	**1750** **Constitutional monarchy**	**1990s** **Democracy**
Parliament's powers	Gave advice, passed laws (usually on the King's orders), consented to taxes		
Royal power	The monarch made all decisions including choosing ministers, and when to summon Parliament		
MPs in the House of Commons	Landowners and rich merchants, unpaid		
House of Lords	Nobles, bishops, abbots, judges		
People with the right to vote	Men who owned or rented property. Landowners could easily influence tenants' votes		
The Government	The King and his Council		

RULERS AND REVOLUTION

William III then arrived in person, and defeated James II and his Irish–French army at the Battle of the Boyne in 1690. James had to escape once again to France.

Religion and land again: The English made the most of their victory. Soon no Catholic could be a lawyer, soldier or MP. All schools and universities were Protestant, and Catholics were not allowed to send their children abroad to be educated in Catholic schools (they did though).

Catholics lost even more land to the English Protestants:

SOURCE 6G

Percentage of Irish land owned by Catholics:

1640: 59%   1658: 22%   1714: 7%

6.19 Draw three pie-charts (circles), each representing 100 per cent, for the three dates given. Colour in the correct sized sector of each circle, to represent land owned by the Irish.

William Hogarth (1697–1764) often painted pictures to show what was wrong in eighteenth-century England, including what went on in elections. Here people are voting at a polling station. Some quite poor people had a vote if they lived in certain houses, but it was difficult for them to make up their minds freely. Landowners who were also MPs often owned these houses, and could make things difficult for the occupants if they voted the wrong way. Candidates often used bribery too, and laid on drunken feasts to win support. Several people in a desperate state have been hauled out here to vote the right way

6.18 What difference did it make that voting was in public, and not secret as it is now?

AT 1.3 3.4

Ireland after 1688

English landowners in London worked out the deal with William and Mary in 1688. Welsh gentry had a small part in it, as they sat in Parliament. But the Irish and the Scots were not consulted at all.

James II hoped he could use Catholic Ireland as a base to win back his kingdom. Louis XIV wanted to cause trouble for William, and gave James a French army, which attacked Protestant Ulster ◁48. James's soldiers surrounded Londonderry and blocked the narrow estuary leading to the town harbour with a boom, so no supplies could get through. The starving Protestant defenders ate rats, mice and candle ends, but they refused to surrender. After 15 weeks, William's ships broke through the boom, and brought in desperately needed food and ammunition. Londonderry was freed.

SOURCE 6H
Pictures like this are often painted on walls in Northern Ireland today

The 'Orange Order' is a group of modern Northern Ireland Protestants who still march today, wearing orange sashes, to celebrate the siege and battle when, as they see it, 'King Billy' (William of Orange) saved them from a 'Papist' take-over. And Catholics in Northern Ireland have never forgotten the injustices which followed the English victory. Events in the Early Modern Age explain much about modern Ireland.

6.20 What kind of people would have painted Source 6H, and why?

AT 3.3 2.2

A WIDER WORLD

Difficult times in Scotland

In Scotland, James II is still called James VII. Like his father and grandfather 79▷ he was also King of Scotland, and many Scots (and some English) still supported him in 1688, especially Catholics in the Highlands. They were called Jacobites (*Jacobus*: Latin for James).

The Highland clans were slow to swear loyalty to William. English troops turned on the Macdonalds in the remote valley of Glencoe. Thirty-six were killed, and many more escaped to the hills and died in the bitter Scottish winter. Several cold wet summers brought bad harvests, and deaths from starvation, even in the more prosperous Lowlands. Scottish trade suffered in the wars with France, and she could not export her cattle, linen and coal. Yet England was growing more prosperous, and Scotland had no share in it.

Then the Scots had a chance to get their own back. When the English Parliament asked the Hanoverian George to rule, the Scots threatened to choose James II's son as their king, and to ally with England's great enemy France, like old times. Reluctantly, the English realised they had to offer the Scots a deal. And also reluctantly, most Scots realised they would do better if they accepted.

The Act of Union, 1707

- The Scots lost their own Parliament.
- Forty-five Scots MPs out of 513 sat in the English Parliament, and 16 lords.
- The Scots kept their Kirk (church), their legal system and their schools – many were better than English ones.
- They could share England's trade and wealth.

The Forty Five

The 'Forty Five' (in 1745) was a serious Jacobite Rebellion. Prince Charles Edward landed from France, took over Edinburgh, and invaded England with his Highland clansmen. But few English risked supporting him, and many Lowland Scots thought they were better off under the Hanoverians. The bitter defeat of Culloden killed Jacobite hopes, and the Highland clans were ruthlessly crushed – even clan tartans and kilts were forbidden. It was not a happy ending, though Scotland grew more prosperous later in the eighteenth century.

SOURCE 6K Prince Charles Edward was James II's grandson 79▷, and Catholic like the rest of his family. At the time of the Forty Five, 'Bonnie Prince Charlie' was a dashing young leader with courage but not much ability, and many Highlanders gave him their enthusiastic loyalty. This portrait of him in middle age shows what defeat, exile, disappointment and drink did to him later

6.21 If Charles Edward had won in 1745 and become King of Great Britain, what differences would you expect to see in Source 6K? *AT 2.5*

6.22 Some people called Charles Edward 'Bonnie Prince Charlie'. Others called him 'The Young Pretender'. Explain the two nicknames. *AT 2.6*

6.23 Make a list in two columns for and against the Act of Union, first by a Scot, and then by an Englishman. Do you think it was fair? *AT 2.8*

6.24 What things make people feel they belong to a particular nation? (For example, why is Highland dress still popular?) *AT 1.7*

Britain was now a United Kingdom – accepted reluctantly by the Scots and the Welsh, and forced on the Irish. But at least it was not a bad thing that all four nations kept their identity and culture, and perhaps some people began to feel 'British'.

7 A wider world

The new London

London's new look after the Fire: a view from the Thames near Westminster by the Italian artist Canaletto in 1753. St Paul's is by far the biggest building (unlike modern London). Its dome rises high above the elegant steeples of the new churches, and the stone houses with tiled roofs. London Bridge is in the distance on the right ◁40, 65

The Great Fire of 1666 gave Londoners a wonderful chance to improve their city. They were lucky too, for they had the right man to plan it for them.

Christopher Wren (1632–1723) was an astronomer, and studied mathematics. He had just begun to design buildings when the Great Fire gave him his chance to become a great architect. Five days after the Fire, he produced a plan which would have made London a beautiful city with wide streets and many open spaces.

The new London did not turn out as Wren planned. Too many people whose houses had been burnt insisted on rebuilding them in the same place, so there were still many narrow crowded streets. All the same, Wren achieved a great deal, including 51 new London churches. His greatest building is St Paul's Cathedral, with its huge dome, which has lasted 300 years, and stood firm during the next fire of London – the air-raids in the Second World War. Wren was buried in St Paul's. The Latin sentence on his tombstone means: 'If you want to see his monument, look around you.'

7.1 Discuss in class: Are we better at planning our cities now? (Think about new buildings, open spaces, traffic problems, fire risks, etc., in your area.)

INVESTIGATION

In what ways was Britain in a wider world by 1750?

Key Sources
- Pictures painted in Britain and India
- Maps
- Records of the Royal Society

Timeline 1600–1750:
- East India Company
- Harvey discovered circulation of blood
- Colony of Virginia founded
- Van Dyck painted Charles I
- Trading base for sugar and slaves set up in Jamaica
- Royal Society
- Last execution for witchcraft in England
- Newton's 'Principia'
- First steam pump
- St Paul's Cathedral finished
- Georgia founded, 13th colony in N. America
- Gainsborough painted Mr and Mrs Andrews

A WIDER WORLD

London life

SOURCE 7A London coffee houses became fashionable meeting places for men from the 1650s. Friends, business men, or politicians met to chat, read the newspapers (which had just started), smoke pipes, and drink coffee

The brewers did not like coffee houses. They produced a pamphlet in 1678 which they said was a petition from women, begging men not to:

SOURCE 7B

trifle away their time, scald their mouths, and spend their money, all for a little base, black, bitter, stinking Puddle Water.

7.2 Were the brewers really worried about what women thought of coffee houses? Why might some wives not like them? *AT 1.3 3.3*

7.3 What evidence do Sources 7A and 7B give about how people drank coffee at first? *AT 3.4*

SOURCE 7C

Drunk for a penny. Dead drunk for tuppence. Clean straw for nothing.

Words over the door of the gin shop, bottom left, Source 7D

7.4 Find more results of gin-drinking in Source 7D. What do the words in Source 7C mean? *AT 3.4*

SOURCE 7D Gin Lane – a poor area of London. Gin was cheap in the early 1700s, and helped people to forget their problems. In this picture of 1751, the artist William Hogarth showed the terrible effects of gin-drinking. For instance, the couple on the left have spent all their money on gin, and have to pawn their cooking pots, and the tools they use to earn a living

Strangers in England

English people called foreigners 'strangers' – there have always been 'strangers' living in Britain, enriching British life with their own culture and talents. The Jews, who were allowed to settle in Britain again by Oliver Cromwell ◀61, came to make a living; there were over 800 in London by 1700, mainly doctors, bankers and merchants. Some strangers came to escape persecution, and others were forced to come.

Black people

SOURCE 7E

We pray you buy for us 15 or 20 lusty young negroes of about 15 years of age, bringing them home with you for London. You will need 30 pairs of shackles and bolts for such of your negroes as are rebellious, and we pray you to be very careful to keep them under, and let them have their food, that they rise not against you, as they have done in other ships.

Part of a letter to a slave ship captain, 1651

THE WIDER WORLD

> **SOURCE 7F**
>
> *A 15 year old boy called John White has run away from Colonel Kirke: he has a silver Collar round his neck, upon which is the Colonel's coat of arms. [1686]*
> *A negro boy called Tony is lost. He has a brass collar on with directions where he lives. [1690]*
>
> Advertisements for runaway slaves in London newspapers

7.5 How useful are Sources 7E, 7F and 7G (below) as evidence of the treatment of black people in seventeenth-century England? *AT 3.6*

Protestant refugees

In Elizabeth I's reign, Protestant refugees fled to England from the war in the Netherlands against Catholic Spain. A group of artists settled in London, including Marcus Gheeraedts, who painted Elizabeth I ◁30.

Louis XIV persecuted French Huguenots (Protestants), and many fled to England, especially after they lost the right to work and worship freely in France in 1685. They were mostly skilled people – clockmakers, silversmiths and doctors. Silkweavers settled in Spitalfields, London, and produced beautiful patterned silk fabrics which were very fashionable.

You may recognise some of these Huguenot names still common in Britain: Bosanquet, Cazenove, Courtauld, De La Mare, Dollond, Faber, Garrick, Lefroy, Millais, Olivier, Savage, Tessier, Vanner.

7.6 Why did the Huguenots find it fairly easy to settle in England and do well? (Notice when they came.) *AT 1.5*

New goods to buy

Rich people like the ones in the coffee houses used many new goods. From the 1650s, sugar became plentiful. It sweetened the fashionable new drinks of tea, chocolate, and the 'Puddle Water', drunk from delicate china bowls (from China) without handles and saucers.

There were new fruits and vegetables: pineapples, tomatoes and potatoes. Tobacco was brought from North America in Elizabeth I's reign, and soon became cheap enough for quite poor people to buy. Pepys ate turkey, another new food ◁62.

Trading ships laden with these goods sailed up the Thames to London. Many goods were exported from London to other parts of Britain and Europe, making the city richer still. Bristol and later Liverpool grew rich on trade from North America and the Caribbean. By 1750, England was a great trading nation.

SOURCE 7G The Duchess of Portsmouth, one of Charles II's mistresses, dressed in the height of fashion. Her pearls, the silk for her dress, and the shift – under-dress – of fine cotton, came from the East. Her black slave girl is wearing these luxury materials too. The Duchess has probably bought her like a piece of property from a slave-ship captain. Do you think she treats the girl well?

A WIDER WORLD

An important visit to the east

SOURCE 7H This Indian artist (his self-portrait is bottom left) shows the power of Emperor Jahangir by his brilliant double halo, dazzling the tiny cherubs above him. But Jahangir is sitting on an hour-glass with the sands running out. He gives a book to a holy Muslim teacher, and does not look at two important rulers, the Sultan of Turkey, and James I of England ◁42

After Sir Thomas Roe's visit, Jahangir gave the East India Company a base in Surat, where they could trade in luxury silks, calico and muslin (two types of cotton material, still luxuries in Europe), rare indigo dyes, and saltpetre, used to make gunpowder.

Gradually merchants set up more bases, and brought in soldiers and guns to defend them. The East India Company grew rich and powerful. The French arrived on the scene (their trading company was founded in 1664), and the Mughal Empire began to break up. The stage was set for a struggle for power and riches between Britain and France which no longer took much notice of the culture of the peoples of India.

The beginning of an empire: By 1750, Britain was a great trading nation. She had settlements in India, and colonies in North America and the Caribbean. In Louis XIV's time, Britain had fought to check French power in Europe ◁63. In the eighteenth century, the two countries fought on land and sea for an empire in India and North America. The Seven Years' War (1756–63) brought victory to Britain in both continents – and a host of future problems.

In 1615 James I sent his ambassador, Sir Thomas Roe, on a mission to the Mughal Emperor Jahangir, who ruled most of northern India. Jahangir's friendship was important – English merchants of the East India Company (founded by Elizabeth I in 1600) were competing for the luxury goods of the East with Portuguese and Dutch traders, and hoped the Emperor would favour them. They were deeply impressed by the riches and civilisation they found in India. Sir Thomas described his first visit to Jahangir's court:

SOURCE 7I

The King sits in a little gallery overhead, covered with canopies of velvet and silk, underfoot laid with good carpets. I delivered his Majesty's letter translated, and my presents were well received. He dismissed me with more favour and grace than was ever shown to any ambassador.

7.7 What messages about Jahangir are in Source 7H?
How can you tell that the artist is Indian (look at the whole picture), but that he has seen western pictures? (Clue: portrait, cherubs.) How might he have done so (Source 7I)?
AT 3.3
AT 3.4

7.8 In Source 7I, what does Sir Thomas think of Jahangir?
AT 3.3

7.9 List the goods mentioned in this section, and mark where they came from on a world map. Put a symbol to show where clashes between European powers over trade were likely.
AT 1.3

7.10 Compare the map opposite with the one on page 7. Which areas were little known in the 1520s, and became centres of British trade by 1750? Think of reasons for this.
AT 1.7

THE WIDER WORLD

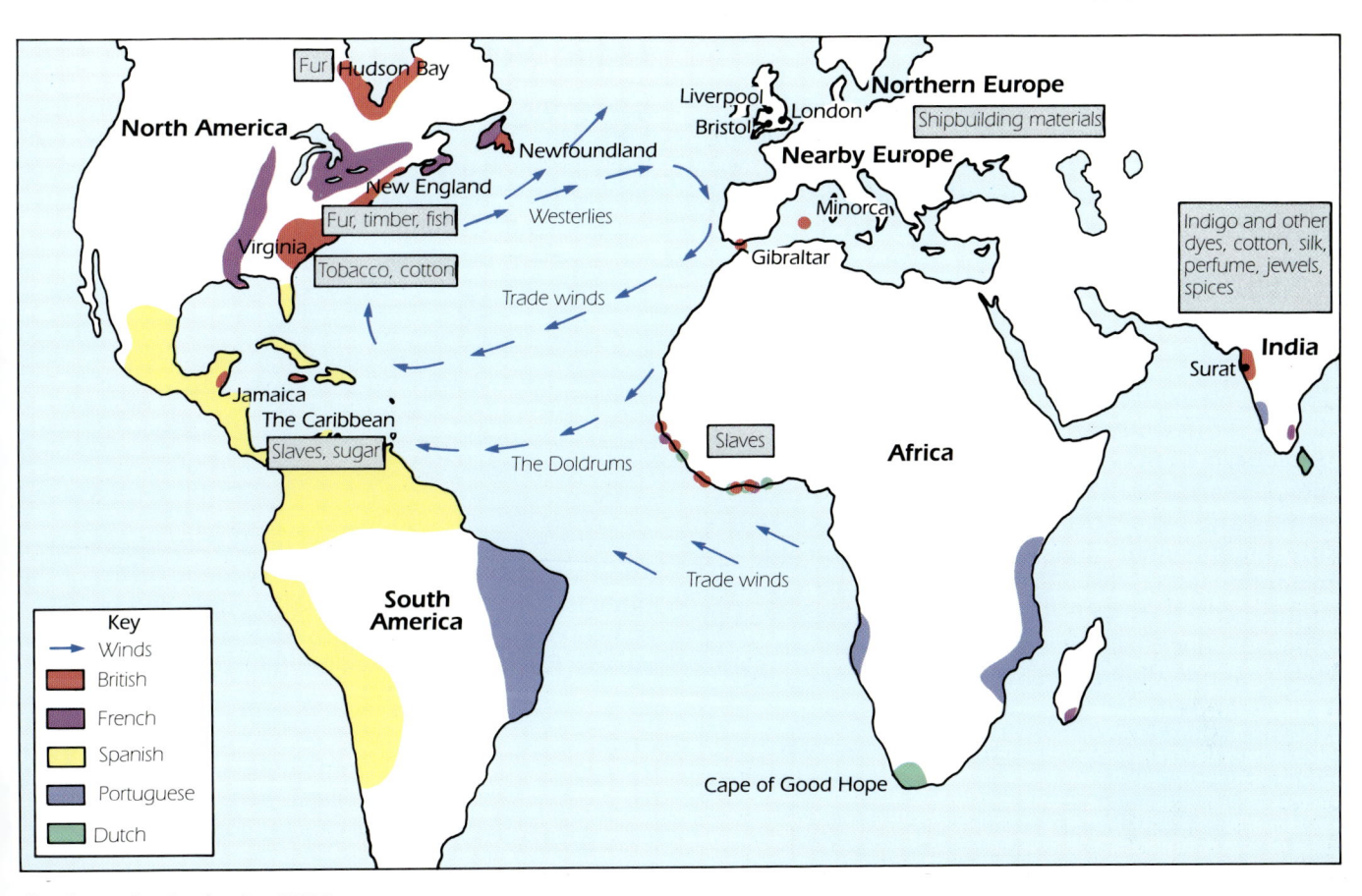

Trade and colonies by 1750

'The great ocean of truth'

People in the Early Modern Age made great discoveries about the world in which they lived. From the 1650s in England, there were important advances in scientific knowledge.

Medicine

William Harvey (1578–1657) discovered in 1616 that the heart worked like a pump, and circulated blood round the body. This was an important step in understanding how the human body worked, but it did little good at the time.

> SOURCE 7J
>
> *After his book on the Circulation of the Blood came out, he lost a great many patients, and 'twas believed he was crack-brained.*
>
> John Aubrey, friend of William Harvey

Harvey did not in fact do too badly – he became tutor to Charles I's sons – but it was a long time before his discovery helped sick people. Doctors went on bleeding and purging ◁52 their unfortunate patients, whatever was wrong with them, until the nineteenth century.

Bubonic plague died out after 1665 ◁65. Smallpox still killed many; there were experiments in vaccination in the 1720s, but it was not until 1796 that Edward Jenner discovered how to use it successfully. Other diseases like tuberculosis could only be cured by luck, and the death rate for mothers and young children remained high. Samuel Pepys was very lucky to survive an operation without anaesthetic to remove a stone as big as a tennis ball from his gall-bladder.

In spite of so much disease, the population continued to rise. More well-built houses of brick and stone, more washable cotton clothes, and a better diet for at least some people probably meant more people lived longer.

7.11 List in two columns: **Changes for the better in health; Continuing problems.** AT 1.6

A WIDER WORLD

The Royal Society

Charles II was very interested in science, and founded the Royal Society in 1662 to encourage all kinds of scientific discovery. Some of the members were interested amateurs like the King and Samuel Pepys, but the Society became important because of the lucky fact that there were so many great scientists working at the time. Some of them, like Christopher Wren ◁71▷ and Robert Hooke, trained at Oxford in Cromwell's time.

The members did experiments and made observations – for instance to see if blood could be transfused from one sheep to another. It could – the bled sheep died, the receiver of the blood was 'strong and lusty'. Unfortunately no one saw that this might benefit humans. They tested the old belief that a spider would not climb out of a circle of unicorns' horns – it did, and they still believed in unicorns' horns! These are some of the inquiries they sent out all over the world in one year, 1666:

> SOURCE 7K
>
> It is altogether necessary to have confirmation of the truth from several people, before they can be relied upon.
> To the East: if diamonds were buried, did they grow again after several years? Whether iron in Japan be better than ours? Whether Japan be truly an island?
> To Virginia and Bermuda: How did the tides work there? Whether a large and beautiful spider ensnared birds?
> To Guinea: Whether the negroes have such sharp sights that they can discover a ship at sea much further off than Europeans can?
> To Egypt: to discover if it ever rained.

SOURCE 7L Robert Hooke designed his own microscope, and used it to make this drawing of a flea – an accurate scientific observation. He also studied optics and astronomy

Isaac Newton

One of the Royal Society's most famous members was Isaac Newton (1642–1723). He left Cambridge early because of the plague in 1665, and continued his study of mathematics at home on his own. His experiments with light convinced him that:

> SOURCE 7M
>
> The most surprising and wonderful composition was WHITENESS. I have often with admiration beheld all the colours of a prism being made to converge, and reproduce light, entirely and perfectly white.

Newton's greatest work was his theory of gravity, and from it he was able to calculate the orbits of the planets. The results were finally published in 1687 in his book *Principia*. Newton became famous and successful, but he always felt he had much more to discover:

> I do not know what I may appear to the world: but to myself I seem to have been only like a boy playing on the seashore, and diverting myself in now and then finding a smoother pebble or a prettier shell than ordinary, while the great ocean of truth lay before me.

7.12 Make a list of the experiments, inquiries and discoveries of the Royal Society in this section, and say which 'school subject' they cover. [AT 3.4]
  a What evidence shows that some scientists were still superstitious? [AT 1.4]
  b What examples show that some scientists were using modern scientific methods? [AT 1.4]
  c How important do you think the scientific discoveries at this time were? [AT 1.6]

Changes for the future

As scientists discovered more of the 'ocean of truth', old superstitions gradually faded away and this had one good result: educated people at least were no longer interested in trials for witchcraft ◁38▷. The last execution for witchcraft in England was in 1686.

In 1698, an engineer called Thomas Savery invented the first steam pump, used to pump water out of coal mines. It was not very efficient and few people at the time knew about it, but it was the first time steam power was used to work machinery. A century later, steam power, and the coal production needed to run it, was turning Britain into a major industrial nation, and changing the lives of British people.

THE WIDER WORLD

Mr and Mrs Andrews

The great artist Thomas Gainsborough (1727–88) was a young man when he painted this superior couple, Mr and Mrs Andrews, soon after their marriage in 1748. They own most of the land in the picture. Mr Andrews has been hunting in his woods, and has given his wife the pheasant he has just shot. But Gainsborough has not finished painting the dead bird – perhaps Mrs Andrews did not like holding it on her beautiful silk skirt

The people you do not see in this picture are important too. Mr and Mrs Andrews and their well-kept land would look very different without the workers in the fields, gardens and stables, and the house servants who cook, clean and wash. These people's lives have changed little since 1500. But a big change lies ahead for everyone, as expansion, trade and industry widens the world still further – the next part of the story of Britain.

Mr Andrews
- Uses new farming methods:
  - Sheep in enclosed fields ◁16▷, so he can breed them carefully, and improve his stock
  - Corn planted in straight rows (perhaps with a new machine called a seed-hopper) and stacked into neat sheaves

  These methods produce more food, but some of his villagers may lose land that they use for their own crops.
- Is probably an MP, and a local magistrate ◁38▷. He enforces laws made in Parliament, and can send poachers in his woods to prison.

Mrs Andrews
- Is 16 years old when this picture was painted
- Is probably not well educated (unlike some Tudor women). May have attended a school for young ladies, and learnt household skills, drawing, dancing and French ◁66▷
- Runs a big household. Will probably spend the next years having children
- Dress: stiff-boned bodice, wide-hooped skirt, high-heeled shoes. Not the dress for an active life – though she may have dressed up for her portrait.

A WIDER WORLD

Summing up: 1500–1750

Living in the Early Modern Age

What have you learnt about people's everyday lives from 1500 to 1750? Copy the table below and fill it in to show what has changed, and what has not changed (continuity), in the lives of Mr and Mrs Andrews compared to Tudor landowners. If you make the table big enough, you can include labelled sketches in some boxes. Use a similar table to show changes and continuity in the lives of ordinary people in country and town. Then discuss which changes you think were improvements, and why.

	Houses	Food	Clothes	Disease	Education	Farming methods
Changes						
Continuity						

The four investigations

Look through this book … what have you learnt about the four investigations suggested on page 7:

Power?   Nationality?   Religion?   A wider world?

Find examples from each of these four topics to answer these questions:

Attainment target 1

Find an example of something which changed over this period.

Why did it change?

What were the results of the change?

Were changes for the better?

Were some more important than others?

What did not change?

How important were people in this change?

Attainment target 2

Find a topic in which there were different views about people or events. Compare the views, and decide why they were different.

Find a topic on which people today still feel strongly, and may disagree. What do you feel about it? Can you decide why you feel this way?

Attainment target 3

Find at least two sources which you think are particularly interesting, and say why.

Find at least two sources which have been useful in providing evidence about events or people.

THE WIDER WORLD

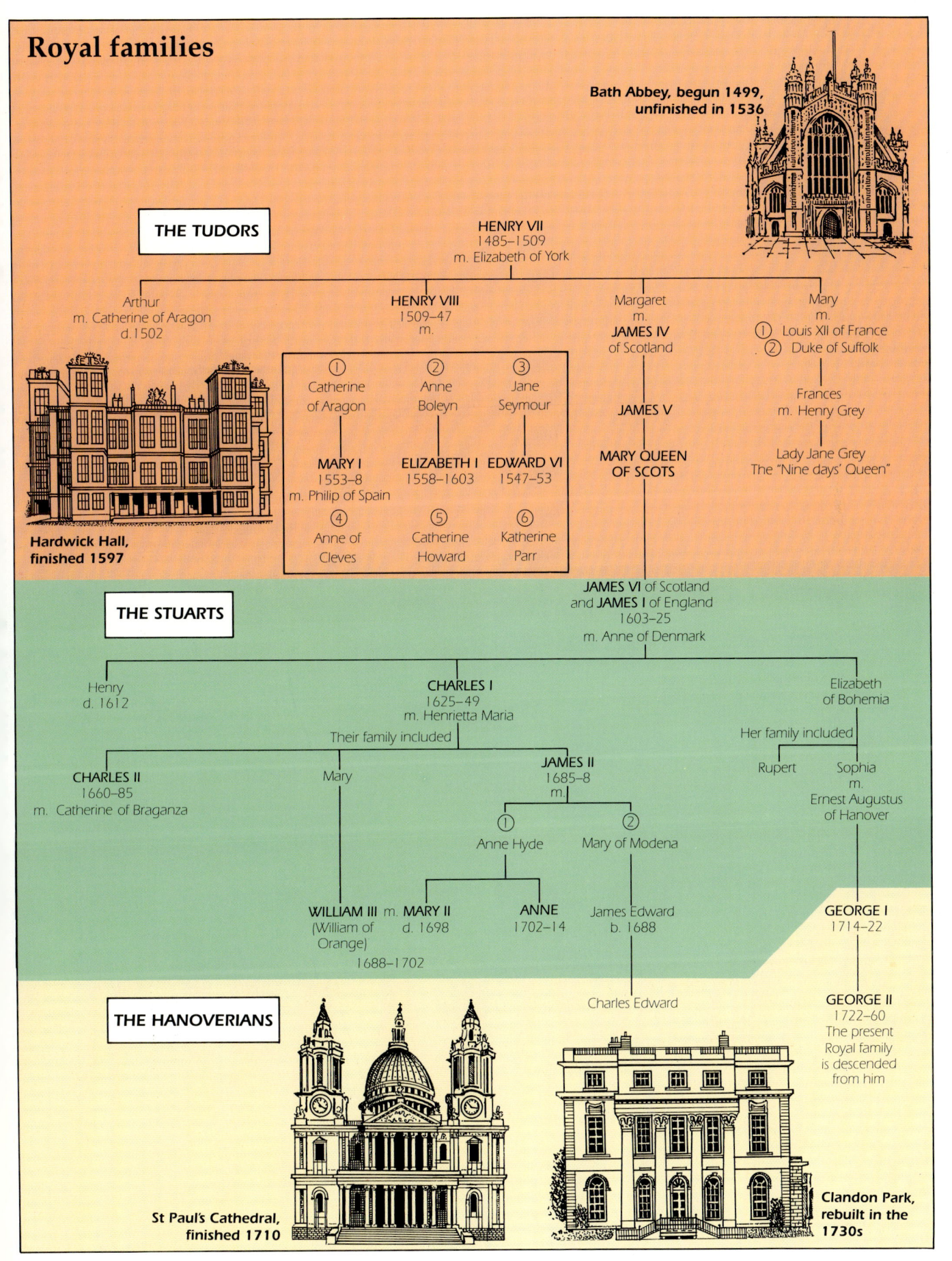

Royal families

Bath Abbey, begun 1499, unfinished in 1536

THE TUDORS

HENRY VII
1485–1509
m. Elizabeth of York

Arthur
m. Catherine of Aragon
d. 1502

HENRY VIII
1509–47
m.

Margaret
m.
JAMES IV
of Scotland

JAMES V

MARY QUEEN OF SCOTS

Mary
m.
① Louis XII of France
② Duke of Suffolk

Frances
m. Henry Grey

Lady Jane Grey
The "Nine days' Queen"

① Catherine of Aragon
② Anne Boleyn
③ Jane Seymour

MARY I
1553–8
m. Philip of Spain

ELIZABETH I
1558–1603

EDWARD VI
1547–53

④ Anne of Cleves
⑤ Catherine Howard
⑥ Katherine Parr

Hardwick Hall, finished 1597

THE STUARTS

JAMES VI of Scotland
and JAMES I of England
1603–25
m. Anne of Denmark

Henry
d. 1612

CHARLES I
1625–49
m. Henrietta Maria
Their family included

Elizabeth of Bohemia
Her family included

Rupert

Sophia
m.
Ernest Augustus of Hanover

CHARLES II
1660–85
m. Catherine of Braganza

Mary

JAMES II
1685–8
m.
① Anne Hyde
② Mary of Modena

WILLIAM III m. MARY II
(William of   d. 1698
Orange)
1688–1702

ANNE
1702–14

James Edward
b. 1688

Charles Edward

GEORGE I
1714–22

GEORGE II
1722–60
The present Royal family is descended from him

THE HANOVERIANS

St Paul's Cathedral, finished 1710

Clandon Park, rebuilt in the 1730s

79

Index and Glossary

Act of Union (Wales), 1536   11, 12
Act of Union (Scotland), 1707   70
alderman, an important townsman on the city council, who chose the Mayor   17
Anne of Cleves   25, 79
Anne, Queen   66–7, 79
apothecary, a shopkeeper who sold medicines, herbs and spices   64–5, 75
apprentice, a boy (occasionally a girl) learning a craft in a seven-year training   17, 21
Armada   36–7

Bankes, Lady   54
Bible   20–1, 28–9, 32–3, 44, 61
Bill of Rights   67
black people   72–3
Boleyn, Anne   18, 19, 24, 25, 79
Bonnie Prince Charlie (*see* Charles Edward)
Book of Martyrs   27
Bosworth, Battle of   10
Bothwell, Earl of   33
Boyne, Battle of   69
Bunyan, John   63

Calvin, Jean   20
castles   12–13
Catherine of Aragon   10, 18, 19, 25, 79
Caxton, William   9
Cecil, Robert   43
Cecil, William   31, 33
Charles I   45–9, 53, 57–8, 79
Charles II   60, 61, 62, 66, 76, 79
Charles V, Emperor   8, 18, 19
Charles Edward   70, 79
children   14–15
Civil War   50–8
clothes   30, 78
coat-of-arms, a family badge in the shape of a shield   12, 72
colony, a place where people from a distant country settled, and took over the land. That country then ruled the colony   44, 74, 75
Commonwealth, the people of England – and the name used for the republic set up after Charles I's execution   57, 60–1
Cranmer, Thomas   19, 26, 27
crime and punishment   38–9, 53, 78
Cromwell, Oliver   56, 57, 59–61
Cromwell, Thomas   19, 22–3, 25

Darnley, Henry   33
democracy, government by all the people   59, 68
dictator, a ruler with absolute (complete) power, who crushes people who disagree with him, and allows no freedom   61
disease and illness   15, 16, 26, 30, 52, 53, 64–5, 75
distaff, a stick to hold raw wool for spinning by hand   15
doctors   6, 16, 52, 75
Drake, Sir Francis   35, 36

East India Company   74
Edgehill, Battle of   50, 51, 52, 56
Edward VI   25, 26, 79
Elizabeth I   19, 28, 30–41, 42, 44, 74, 79
empire, a group of countries ruled by a great power   35
enclosures   16, 25, 78
epidemic, a widespread outbreak of an infectious disease   16
Evelyn, John   62, 67
excommunicate, to expel someone from the Church, and condemn them to Hell   34
explorers   7, 8

farming   15, 16, 78
Fawkes, Guy   43
Fire of London   65, 71
Flodden, Battle of   13
food   6, 36, 72

'Forty-five, The'   70
Foxe, John   27

Gainsborough, Thomas   78
games   6, 41
gentry, landowners who came next to nobles in importance and wealth   11, 14, 68
George I   67, 68, 79
George II   68, 79
government, the person or people who hold power, and rule a country   11, 58
Grey, Lady Jane   26
guilds   17
Gunpowder Plot   43

Hampden, John   46
Harvey, William   75
Hawkins, Sir John   35
heir, the person who will be the next king or queen, or will take over property when the present owner dies   66
Henrietta Maria   45, 49, 79
Henry VII   10, 12, 79
Henry VIII   4, 7, 10–11, 13, 18–26, 79
heretic, a person who refuses to accept the official teaching of the Church   27, 34
Hogarth, William   68, 72
Holbein   4, 16, 18, 19, 24
Hooke, Robert   76
Howard, Catherine   25, 79
Huguenots   73
Hutchinson, Lucy   52, 54

Ireland   7, 12, 37, 48, 60, 61, 69, 70

Jahangir   74
James IV of Scotland   10, 32, 79
James I of England and VI of Scotland   33, 42, 43, 44, 74, 79
James II of England and VII of Scotland   63, 66–7, 69, 70, 79
James Edward   67, 79
Jews   61, 72

Knox, John   32

Laud, William,   47, 48
Leicester, Earl of   31
Leonardo da Vinci   8, 9
Levellers   59
London   16, 27, 38, 40, 49, 56, 64–5, 66, 67, 71–2, 73
Louis XIV   63, 67, 69, 73, 74
Luther, Martin   20

Margaret Tudor   10, 12, 13, 79
Marston Moor, Battle of   51, 55
martyr, a person who dies for his or her beliefs   27, 34
Mary I   18, 25, 26–7, 28, 79
Mary II   62, 63, 66, 67, 69, 79
Mary Queen of Scots   32–4, 35, 79
Mary Rose   4–6
mass, the most important Catholic service, celebrating the last supper Jesus had with his disciples before his death   29, 34
Mayflower   44
medicine   6
Michelangelo   20
monasteries   22–3
More, Sir Thomas   24
music   41

Naseby, Battle of   51, 56
New Model Army   56
Newton, Sir Isaac   77
Nonconformists   63, 67
nunneries   22

Pale, the   11
parish, a district with its own church and clergyman   29

Parliament   11, 18, 19, 21, 25, 34, 42, 43, 46–9, 59, 60–1, 66, 67
Parr, Katherine   25, 79
Penn, William   63
Pepys, Samuel   62, 64, 65, 75, 76
Philip of Spain   26, 27, 28, 31, 35
pilgrimage, a journey to a holy place   12
Pilgrimage of Grace   25
Pilgrim Fathers   44
Pilgrim's Progress   63
physician, a top-ranking doctor, trained in Latin, Greek, astronomy and philosophy   61
plague, usually means bubonic plague, spread by rat fleas   16, 64–5
plays   40
Poor Law   39
population   16, 40
poverty and the poor   38–9, 59
Presbyterians   32, 66
printing   9
privilege, a special right or advantage given to someone   46
propaganda, information giving one viewpoint, often put out by a government to win support   66
punishment   (*see* crime)
Puritans   44, 47, 50, 51, 61, 62, 63
Pym, John   49

Quakers   59

Reformation   20
relic, part of a holy person's body or belongings, kept after their death in a holy place. Some relics were fakes   20
Renaissance   8, 20
republic, a country which is not ruled by a king   63
rosary, beads used by Catholics to guide their prayers   6
Rupert, Prince   55, 56

Scotland   12–13, 32–3, 42, 47, 57, 60, 69, 70
Seymour, Jane   25, 79
ship money   46, 48
ships   4–6, 12, 36–7
shrine, a holy place. Often a relic was kept there   12
Strafford, Earl of   48
superstition, the belief that certain things we do (e.g. touching wood) will guard us from bad luck   20
surgeon, a less important doctor. He performed operations, and was often a barber as well   6, 52

theatre   40
Tories   66
towns   17
trade   17, 35, 63, 70, 73–4
traitor, someone who betrays his or her country   57
treason, plotting against the King or Queen   19, 34
typhus, a dangerous infectious illness spread by body lice, usually in dirty, crowded conditions   16
tyrant, a cruel ruler with complete power   57

Verney family   50

Wales   7, 11, 12, 21, 70
Walpole, Robert   68
Walsingham, Sir Francis   34
weapons   6, 8, 36, 52
Wesley, John   63
Whigs   66
William of Orange   63, 67, 69, 79
Wolsey, Thomas   19, 24
women   15, 18, 21, 38, 52, 54, 72, 78
Wren, Sir Christopher   71, 76